STREETLIFE

Barbara Gibson

LUME BOOKS

LUME BOOKS

This edition published in 2022 by Lume Books

ISBN 978-1-83901-497-0

Typeset using Atomik ePublisher from Easypress Technologies

www.lumebooks.co.uk

Table of Contents

Author's Note

The oral histories presented in this book were recorded in 1993 and 1994, and are now historical documents. These are stories told from the interviewees' own perspectives, in their own language and reflecting their culture at that time. They show us how these people were marginalized in so many ways – through homophobia, transphobia, racism, prejudice against those selling sex and for being perceived vectors of HIV. They were let down by their parents, caregivers, the services they encountered and even the laws that had been put in place to protect them. Their stories highlight the consequences of the isolation, marginalization and lack of understanding they faced.

Readers should be aware that the tone and content in some parts of this book reflect attitudes that are today regarded as transphobic, homophobic, racist and/or 'anti-sex work'. The self-deprecating humour of that time is no longer funny, and may be shocking to many. These historic records should now be viewed as a mark of the moral progress that has been made, how situations have progressed and what further work still needs to be done. Above all, it is not my intention to distress or offend.

A note from the author on language
It is not my intention to trivialize or to appear derogatory in using terms such as 'rent boy,' 'boy' and 'punter' in my writing. I have retained these words to reflect the historical context of this book at the time it was first written. The word 'transsexual' was also commonly used during this period although I have replaced this with 'trans' in my text. However, I have kept the slang and cultural

language references exactly as they were told to me, to preserve the authentic voices.

Notably, the British Library amplifies the importance of these historical records in the following words (https://sounds.bl.uk/Oral-history/Law, accessed 16.06. 2022):

Oral history recordings provide valuable first-hand testimony of the past. The views and opinions expressed in oral history interviews are those of the interviewees, who describe events from their own perspective. The interviews are historical documents and their language, tone and content might in some cases reflect attitudes that could cause offence in today's society.

What the interviews tell us
One-to-one oral history interviews explore memories and recount narratives in ways rarely found elsewhere. Personal testimony fills knowledge gaps, provides new insights, challenges stereotypical views and overturns orthodoxies. These recordings reveal collective memory, individual agency, gender, skill, influence and intentionality.

Ethical use of oral history
The interviewees have been generous in sharing their memories – often traumatic, confidential and intimate – and listeners [readers] are asked to treat this material with respect and sensitivity, and consider it in context, so that the interviewees' meanings are not misconstrued.

Acknowledgements

My heartfelt thanks to the individuals who have freely given their time, trust and commitment to the creation of this book. Without the courage they have shown in sharing their feelings and intimate details of their lives, and their unfailing enthusiasm, this project would never have gotten off the ground. My thanks, too, to other Streetwise youths who have generously shared their stories with me: I am grateful to them all.

My thanks, too, to the many people who gave me their time in many ways during the first publication of this book in 1995, including my consultants Simon Watney, Dr José Catalán (reader in psychiatry, Charing Cross and Westminster Medical School) and Orville Hemans. Other people and organizations gave me professional advice: The Children's Society, Barnardos' Sold-It team, Release, Judy Tavanyar, Professor Sylvia Chant, Niamh Cullen, Father Bill Kirkpatrick (co-founder of Streetwise Youth), Tony Whitehead (former director of Streetwise Youth), Melissa Agar, Caroline Lees, Madser's partner and Steven Devote.

Thanks to Rachel Morton for her endless support and patience. Also, thanks to Peter Hughes, the Praed Street Project, friends and family for their constant encouragement.

Special thanks to Caroline Montgomery, my agent at Rupert Crew Ltd, and to Cassell, my original publisher, for having the confidence in me, and giving me the opportunity to launch my first book.

Many thanks for the additional help I received for this 2022 edition, from Associate Professor Ford Hickson, Dr Wendy Rickard, Tony Whitehead, Verena Tschudin, Jane Ayres, Chez Dhaliwal, Del

Campbell, Michelle Ross, Ford Hickson, Fergal McCullough, Tanya Smith, Sarah Gibson.

And finally, special thanks again to Caroline Montgomery, and to James Faktor of Lume Books for making this edition possible.

Introduction

I first walked through the doors of Streetwise Youth's safe house in 1988. It was opposite the cemetery on the Old Brompton Road, in Earl's Court, London. A small, shabby, two-bedroom flat on the top floor of a three-storey building. The crowded, smoke-filled living room was the drop-in, occupied by around ten rent boys and Zoe, who identified herself to me as a 'pre-op transsexual'. The atmosphere was boisterous, emotionally and sexually charged, full of colourful banter. Two exhausted youths, who had been up all night with nowhere to stay, had crashed out on the shabby sofa. A member of staff was sitting at a table helping a flamboyantly dressed young person find emergency accommodation. A volunteer, sitting on the floor in the corner of the room, was supporting a boy in distress. The previous night his punter had deliberately, and without consent, discretely removed a condom during penetrative sex. Not only had he been potentially exposed to HIV and other sexually transmitted diseases, this was rape, too.

Streetwise was set up in 1985. A ground-breaking charity, it provided non-judgemental counselling, help and support to marginalized males and trans women aged between 16 and 25 who sold sex, or exchanged sex for goods or a bed for the night. They were commonly called 'rent boys', 'boys', 'street prostitutes', 'survival sex workers', 'bum boys', 'boys on the game', 'young adults who sold sex on the streets'. These different terms reflected judgemental, respectful or cultural attitudes. They were labelled as immoral or perverts due to the taboo natures of both selling sex and having sex with men. Behind their veneer of bravado, these youths were needy and demanded a lot of attention, often in a provocative, confrontational manner. They were at the vulnerable end of the sex work spectrum. They were at the vulnerable end of homelessness too – for other homeless people looked down on those who sold sex. Streetwise provided a unique, welcoming environment where they could talk openly about their sex work and the rest of their problems. As well as responding to crises such as assault and rape, the charity offered advice about healthcare, drugs, housing and welfare rights. It provided meals and showers – all available as a 'one stop shop' under its small roof. There was also an outreach and a helpline service.

I was employed to develop specialized HIV/AIDS health education, support and resources. This was the time when rising numbers of people were dying with AIDS and the first antiviral drug, zidovudine (AZT), was just becoming available, although that carried its own considerable side effects. Sadly, some of our clients had already contracted HIV which was seen by some as a death sentence. Streetwise aimed to help these young people, who lacked self-worth, build their self-esteem. For some, becoming infected with the virus paled into insignificance when weighed against the other problems they were facing or had faced. Contracting the virus gave them rapid access to housing, benefits and care. For some, this was the means to get what they needed. Another priority for the charity was to help its clients reduce their exposure to harm by enabling them to develop skills to creatively negotiate sex safely and change the power dynamics of their encounters. Punters were seen to have the upper hand as they had the money these youths needed. Some punters were violent or demanded unsafe sex – putting our clients at high risk of contracting HIV and other sexually transmitted diseases, as well physical, psychological and emotional abuse. They found themselves 'consenting' to activities they did not want to engage in, or did not even know existed until too late.

I found quiet spaces inside or outside the day centre to set up one-to-one sessions with these individuals. 'Having an HIV talk' gave the opportunity to identify their unique problems and to work with them to stay safe and well. I accompanied them to collect their HIV results from the nearby John Hunter Clinic, part of the Chelsea and Westminster Hospital, on the Fulham Road. Our walks back through the cemetery were either joyful or tearful depending on the results. We had many a crisis counselling session in a quiet spot amongst the gravestones.

I worked alongside another team member at night. We went into the areas where punters would find the rent boys. The boys would come up to us only too glad to see a friendly face; they asked for condoms, help and advice, or to let off steam. Sometimes we bought them a hot drink at Dunkin Donuts, to discuss a pressing problem. It was here they introduced us to the 'newbies' on the streets, so we could let them know what help was available to them. Some of the boys were dressed in the only bedraggled clothes they owned, others were provocatively dressed, emphasising their boyishness – they were often the ones to hit the gay clubs later. They were out at night, sometimes all night, whatever the weather, in the freezing cold and rain.

Our outreach sessions began in the early evening at Victoria railway station. Here we found them looking for business as they discreetly mingled amongst the busy commuters returning home from work. We would then go on to the backstreets of Piccadilly, also known as the 'Dilly' or the 'Meat Rack'. And finally on to Soho, ending the night in the infamous Golden Lion pub – historically known as a haunt for punters and rent boys.

It was essential for us to keep a low profile on the station and streets. We respected that they were working. We were all on our guard against drawing attention to ourselves, and dodging the undercover police. If apprehended, they regularly had their condoms confiscated, were charged with highway obstruction or, worse still, for importuning – the legal term for which is now soliciting.

Streetwise was really like entering another world. As I got to know these people, I understood how they had been unjustly marginalized and criminalized. I was surprised to find out how much they had already experienced in their short lives. Most had been seriously neglected and let down by their families, carers and local authorities. Many bore the scars of abuse. For them, life had been so intolerable, they were left with little option but to run away at a very early age.

Generally arriving in London, with nowhere to live and no idea of where to go for help, they had few choices and would inevitably resort to the only resource they had – their bodies. Selling sex became their best option for survival, when weighed against the few legal alternatives available to them. But it wasn't simply about money – selling sex served many other purposes; it was a source of affection, attention, fun and adventure, and often provided a place to stay at night. It could also serve to reinforce patterns of abuse.

The criminal nature of this activity meant that the boys were driven underground and formed a subculture of their own. Behind their veneer of bravado, they had few expectations of life and couldn't go anywhere for help. Their childhood experiences meant they had a mistrust of services and the law. But they discovered through their peers that Streetwise's non-judgemental approach was different. Its services were trusted, popular and, over the years, saw hundreds of young males and a few young trans women through its doors and on the streets. The project grew rapidly, and in around 1991 moved into a newly refurbished, spacious house at 11 Eardley Crescent. More drop-in staff were taken on and the newly-expanded outreach team was supported by Barnardo's child protection charity.

I had five amazing years working alongside these young people, until 1993 when we were all made redundant. Streetwise was closed down for a service and funding review, leaving about 150 young males and trans women with very little support. Barnardo's set up Sold-It to provide continuity with the outreach service. Streetwise Youth later made a limited comeback, but was then restructured into SW5, which was then remodelled into SWISH. During the downsizing processes, the charity's independent status was lost, and the drop-in and essential services considered necessary for the survivor sex worker disappeared too. No such dedicated service exists in London now.

In recent years, the scene has changed. Sex work is conducted via mobile phone apps and this has improved the lives of some who choose to sell sex and who have the life skills and safe environment to do so. But, sadly, the more vulnerable slip through the net. The great news for many sex workers is the availability of PrEP, the game-changing drug which, if taken as prescribed, is highly effective at preventing HIV – although not other sexually transmitted diseases. But for those who are homeless, accessing a prescribing service and remembering to take the pill as required, is most unlikely.

The arrival of these apps has also meant people can easily hook up with like-minded others for free, without the risks of procuring sex on the streets. This has led to a reduced demand for these youths in their traditional haunts – they have moved to gay venues or into more dangerous, isolated environments.

After the demise of Streetwise, I asked four young males – Madser, Paul, Ryan and Adam – and two young trans women – Zoe and Simone – if they would be interested in helping me create a book of their life stories in return for practical and emotional support. During the time I had known them, they had gained some stability in their lives and I could record them in the comfort of their homes. All willingly agreed, feeling it would be very therapeutic and life affirming for them. They recognized the importance of having their voices made public, to help others understand their situations better. My aim was to invite the reader into their lives, to get a glimpse of their world, their thoughts and beliefs.

There is virtually no first-hand documentary literature on this subject from this time, academic or otherwise. I am one of few people who has been able to build relationships of trust with these people and was ideally placed to write about their lives. They knew I would believe what they had to say and would not judge or exploit them.

I drew up a written contract with each person, to include details such as mutually respecting confidentiality. I made it clear that I would not include any information that I had gained about them through my work at Streetwise, and I would use only information obtained in our interview sessions. Their stories were captured on audio tape and transcribed. The transcriptions were condensed to create the chapters in this book.

The whole process of putting this book together was very emotionally demanding for all involved. Sometimes 'book sessions' were replaced by crisis counselling. Early in the preparation of this book, as a result of other things going on in their lives, four of the contributors were deeply suicidal. However, all experienced a recovery of hope and were insistent on continuing with our recordings.

They recounted vivid descriptions of their rollercoaster lives: mixed emotional memories from their childhood, family life and experiences in local authority care. They spoke frankly about their emerging sexuality, changing sexual identities, and for Zoe and Simone, the manifestation of their trans identities. There are painful stories of abuse, racial abuse too. They revealed in colourful detail what led them to sell sex, what they did, where, for how much, what their punters were like and how selling sex affected them. They gave eye-opening accounts of how their lifestyles afforded excitement, sometimes shocking adventures, excessive drug and alcohol use. They gave insights into their good and bad relationships, their friendships and times of loneliness and isolation. They remembered the darker sides of their lives, their experiences with mental health, HIV, dealing with the pressures to have safe or unsafe sex. What emerged were stories of incredible resilience and extraordinary strength.

All the accounts in this book are told using their own words from the recordings undertaken in 1993 and 1994. But I have changed their names and certain locations to keep the interviewees' identities, their families and associates anonymous. I have retained the slang and the cultural language references of that time. I hope that by reading these life stories the reader will be better able to accept and understand why these young people led the lives they did. I would also like to feel that the 'whole' person may be perceived, instead of the focus being purely on their sexual activities and thus perpetuating the image for which they have been so frequently stigmatized and misunderstood.

There were lots of joyous and humorous times in our various relationships, which slowly changed my role from professional worker to something akin to an older sister. I thought our friendships would continue. But they didn't.

Madser died with AIDS in 1994. He insisted on continuing to record his life story right until the end of both his story and his life, motivated by the fact that he would be leaving something for posterity.

Paul died with AIDS in 1995, a year after he had finished his recordings, having returned home to spend the last few months of his life with his mum.

Tragically, Zoe was found dead in bed after seeing a punter at her home in 1996.

Adam had made it clear that he wanted to do his recording as closure on this chapter of his life. He moved on to caring work.

Ryan and Simone eventually lost contact with me. I do not know what became of them.

I wish to thank them all so much for placing their trust in me and being so candid about their lives. Their voices and stories are captured on audio recordings as oral history. They are secured for posterity in the British Library Sound Archive.

'Out on the Streets'

Why do I sit here night after night?
In the cold under the street light,
Cold and alone. I just can't cope,
I feel like shit, I want to go to my mum and home.
I need some money, it must be tonight,
I'm starving hungry, some food would be nice.
I need a punter please right now.
Is that one hanging about?
Do I approach him, can it be right?
He could be a cop, he's been there all night.
I think I'll just leave it, I'll just walk around.
He's looking at me. I can't work it out.
It would be just my luck if I got nicked tonight.
Where's that guy gone who was looking at me?
Oh shit, he's gone off with another queen.
What a cheek! He's already done three.
Quick, someone else is looking at me.
Get in there quick, it's getting late.
He smiles at me, 'Business darling?',
'You ugly queen, what a state!'
I'll have to do him. I have no choice.
I desperately need the cash and some food to eat.
We'll go back to his flat and it's really late.
This is the bit I really hate:

1

He's touching and hugging me, wanting me,
Begging me, dying to fuck me.
'Sorry mate, no one does that to me of late;
No matter what you say or pay.
Whatever we do, it must be safe.'
He pushes me down on the bed,
To suck his pathetic excuse for a dick.
I feel really sick; but what can I say.
I hope he comes soon. I can't take much more today.
I can't get a hard-on for which he desires.
I'm much too tired.
He's finally coming at last.
Thanks to my charm and powerful arm.
He pays me money saying I'm great.
When I count it, it's not so great.
I'm £20 short. He says he's broke.
There's nothing to do but escape.
I'm too tired to get in a state.
So off I go, at last I'm free.
I could eat a pizza for four!
I didn't get nicked, that's a relief.
To appear in court would cause me grief.
I don't want a record or prison spell
To make my life hell.
I want to be free.
It's just not me
Selling my body out on the streets.
With no money and nothing to eat.

Contributed by Ryan

'Madser'

Me ma nearly died when she gave birth to me on Fireworks Night in 1969. She'd already lost twins in pregnancy between me and me older brother and then things went wrong after me conception. I don't know what was wrong with her, she was bleeding a lot internally and it was maybe too late to get any help in time. Luckily for us, an off-duty doctor who lived over the road saved us. I was born with a streak of hair down to me shoulder and I cried all the time. I think me ma always resented me for the bad time that I gave her.

Me ma and da came to Birmingham to get work. They had family there. Me da was a self-employed road builder but the work ran out and, just before me second birthday, they moved back to Dublin with Sean me older brother, Tom me younger brother and meself, to be near me grandparents.

I haven't got many memories of me early childhood because I have blanked most of it. I've found in me life I've had a lot of blanks. I've tried to think why; it seems to be easier to block things out. I do remember every evening there was screeching going on downstairs and plates banging on the walls because me ma and da were arguing all the time because he was drunk. Me ma provoked him by calling him a drunken bastard and he would give her a good hiding. I'd come down in the morning and there would be broken plates, hair and everything all over the place.

I was living on me nerves watching me ma and waiting for her to start on me. She would find any excuse to take it out on me; it could happen just by saying anything, making a comment about helping to wash the dishes. I'm sure she didn't know what she was doing, she needed a scapegoat and what was happening to her, she was repeating on me nearly every day. I was beaten up black and blue. When I was five, I remember one of me brothers got a racing-track game for Christmas. It had yellow flexible tracks which could be arranged round in big circles. They were big, long, yellow tracks and I used to get beaten stupid with them. When the track hit me across me back I would rush and hide under the bed and then I would get the handle of the hairbrush smack against me head while she called me an evil little bastard. Me ma would always use some form of weapon or other; more hairbrushes went snap over me head than I've had hot dinners. She didn't like me younger brother, John, either but she didn't take it out on him as much.

I knew me da loved me because he always made sure we had plenty of clothes and food. I was very close to me four brothers and sister. They would come upstairs to me room and try to protect me, and Sean would sneak food up to me when I was not allowed to eat following a beating. We all grew up together, hung around with each other and trusted each other.

When I was three, me ma took me to me first day at school where all the other kids were crying, they didn't want their mammies to go. For me it seemed like freedom, and the next day I went on me own. I got lost, but then found me way. The school was run by nuns, penguins, they were running the shop. They always seemed to be snapping at me, I hated being told what to do all the time and I became disruptive. I was leaving me house with the shit there and then ending up in the shit at school. I ended up kicking the nuns.

Unlike other kids, our family never went away on holiday. From around the time I was three, we went out on day trips to the amusement arcades and all the family done the machines. I was not allowed out of mammy's and daddy's sight because if I moved – BANG, I'd get slapped about me head. I learned a lot watching me ma and da play, and by the time I was seven I was playing them on me own. I used to slip in and out of the arcades and no one noticed me. When I played the machines I escaped, I forgot about everything, I went into a trance. I'd often blow £100 and get it back. I became hooked on them. I got the money from doing the milk rounds which I started around the same age.

Before going to school, Sean and I would be up at five o'clock in the morning and meet the milkman to do the milk round with him. We got paid 50p a week and got tips for helping to collect the money. I wanted money as there was never enough of it about. On the round we used to find cars lying around which shouldn't have been there. We knew who all the local cars belonged to, so these must have been stolen. We learned how to get in and out of them. Through pure devilment we learned to take the radios and other bits and used to flog them. As we got older we had it so well organised we made a lot of money. We were too young to have so much money and so we paid the milkman to look after it for us in his bank account. We were clever: if we walked into a shop with a £20 note for sweets they would be wanting to know where it came from, so we always made sure we had change. I spent the money on sweets, sometimes fags for me ma, and I started smoking, and of course I had as much money as I wanted for the fruit machines.

At the age of seven, I thought I was learning to take care of meself. Me ma always had this thing that she wasn't always going to be there for us, and that you would have to learn to do things for yourself. I now had learned to make money and I was learning to try to please me ma because there was less chance of getting a slap. Me ma wasn't a very good cook and I started cooking for the family. I used to cook childish things like fish fingers, sausages and eggs, I could also cook a coddle or a stew, I learned to check the roast in the oven. I was never thanked for doing it, I think it was appreciated but I still got beaten.

I believed me ma thought I was evil: as I was getting me head punched in, she would shriek, 'I'll make you regret the day you were born you evil bastard.' She said that throughout me life. As I got older I blamed the things that happened in me life on her. That statement has always played on me mind, even now. As a child I wanted to die, there were these children's homes around where I was living and I'd see the guys there getting better cared for than I did, they had pool tables and television.

Learning the Catechism to make your first Holy Communion was automatic at me school. I went to the special classes when I was six years old and learned a rhyme. By taking the first letter of each word I could spell Catechism backwards: 'Master Sits In His Chair Each Time At Catechism'. I didn't understand why I had to learn this, I was never too much into religion anyway. Taking your first Communion in the Catholic Church was a special ceremony, I had me 'religious experience' when I got me money afterwards. We were given gifts of money and I made thirty-six quid, a heck of a lot of money in those days. One neighbour gave me an apple as a present, I bit into it and out came me first tooth!

We also got money at Halloween. Curly kale was boiled up with potatoes and they were mashed together and then for a treat there were coins wrapped up in pieces of foil and stuck inside the vegetables and we'd get whatever was served up in our portion. We loved Halloween, we used to dress up and go around trick-or-treating, begging for apples or oranges as was the tradition.

Because of me family moving to another house in Dublin, I changed school at the age of seven. They had already heard about me disruptive reputation. I was a very fast learner, I learned so fast that I couldn't sit easy and so I disrupted the class. Me teacher used to lock me in the classroom at break and lunch times. He could not try to understand why I was being disruptive. Rather than try and understand why I was wild and hyper, they locked me in the library, and then I got so angry I would pull that apart and then I was taken into the headmaster's class. I used to like that because I would stand there facing the wall, listen and learn. By the age of nine, I learned that things were better when I was out 'on the mitch' [truanting].

As a kid, I'd read 'Dan Dare', 'Robin Hood' and 'The Famous Five', and from these I learned to create me own adventures while I was on the mitch. Rather than be the goody-goody, which I couldn't be since I believed I was an evil bastard, I was the little baddy. I was always fighting other kids; that's when I got me nickname 'Madser', meaning 'little hard nut' in Irish. I was the leader of me brothers and friends. I spent the time masterminding the plans for nicking things, burglaries and ways of making money. It played on me conscience that I was hurting innocent people, maybe I was making them regret the day they were born, I hoped I was making me ma and da regret the day they were born. They wanted a little bastard, they treated me like one and so they'd have one – but I was going to be the little bastard who was *not* going to regret the day he was born. Looking back, I saw how they treated me and used situations to abuse other people.

I was surprised I made me Confirmation because you have to attend school every day for six months to learn all your religious stuff. They don't let you take your Confirmation unless you've been practising your Catechism and so I was surprised I made mine because I hadn't done either. There were other girls and a lad who were asked to leave the Church because they hadn't satisfied the conditions.

I made me Confirmation with me younger brother Tom when I was ten years old, in a blue suit, he was in a brown suit. I had a blue suit for me Holy Communion too. Me mammy must have had a thing about me in blue suits. After the ceremony, it was customary for people to say you look nice, touch your suit and hand you the dosh. I think that was the most important part of the day, we made a fortune.

Around this time I used to pop into the convent at lunchtimes because they used to do free meals for homeless people. I got to know this older guy who I'd seen around who done a window-cleaning job. I never paid much attention to him until, one day, he asked me to help him with this window-cleaning job, but he wanted me to help him steal a bike first. We went down to the docks, lifted a bike and on the way back he took me on a short cut. He stopped off at this trailer thing and innocently I followed him in. He then made me give him a blow job. I didn't really know what I was doing, I knew in me own little way it wasn't right. After he'd come I just ran off, but there wasn't a place I could run to, I wanted to run home but I was on the mitch and I had put meself into this situation. I went back to the cattle yard, one of me private haunts. I was in a bit of a spot, I thought; upset, confused and in turmoil. I tried to blank me feelings.

When I met him again I just blanked him; later I started resenting and hating him. I wouldn't like the fucker to have done it to anyone else. I wasn't going to take it to heart, not like the beatings that were still going on in me life. It wasn't until I got older that I realized after reading all the things in the newspapers that I actually knew it was sexual abuse and it was wrong. At the particular time I was none the wiser about what had happened, sex wasn't talked about at home let alone between two men.

When I was eleven years old, a particular teacher always harassed me, and used to beat me. No one paid any attention because it always seemed to be just me and me friends and everyone else thought we deserved it. One day the teacher hit a mate of mine in the class, and so I picked up a chair, and hit the teacher with it. Then there were four of us on the teacher; me, me mate, his brother and me brother. I then walked out of the school for good. Later I got transferred to a school run by the Christian Brothers. Afterwards it came to light that other kids were beaten up by the teacher, and the school closed down.

I was OK for the first week after me transfer, but then, as I was the new guy, I got involved in a lot of fights. People didn't like me and I didn't like them. Shortly after I'd been there, the principal from the last school came up to me new school and had words with them about me and from then on me life was made a misery again. Me teacher regularly got so annoyed with me, he chased me around the classroom and so I'd leave for the day.

I was expelled from the Christian Brothers' school because of me absences. I then went to the technical college when I was twelve. I continued to go on the mitch. Me absence from school was never properly investigated. I thought they must have been happier when I wasn't there, I always caused problems and I was a right little evil bastard when I was there. As I got older I spent periods of three to six months on the mitch at any given time.

Eventually I was referred to see a child psychologist; me ma and da were a bit sceptical about it but they agreed anyway, and me ma was called in with me. I was asked why I was so disruptive and wouldn't learn

8

anything. I said it was because I already knew what was being taught, I was a very bright kid and they didn't know that. The psychologist laughed at me and put me to the test. Every question he asked I answered. At the end he laughed again. I don't understand what happened but it was decided that I should be transferred to another school.

I was a wild child, and me da and ma wouldn't have this, they decided to keep me at home and give me a set amount of work to do. I always done it. The schools weren't doing me any good and were restricting me in me abilities. I had finished school at the age of twelve and I wanted a real job. I used to go round for jobs and convince them I was fifteen. I used to con them, I would sit there and carry on in the interview and keep a straight face, I had the bottle. When they used to find out I was only twelve they used to give me money for trying!

I started to take orders for things to steal. Me brothers and I would get plaster boards from the local gypsum factory up the road, wood from the local wood factory and we went along the train track for coal. We took orders for whatever was needed and made a lot of money.

Me da started building a bigger kitchen for me ma and he ran out of money. Me ma was really pissed off. I found out what was needed and Sean, Tom and me got the plaster boards and wood which was found in the garden next morning. No one ever mentioned a word about it.

When I heard me ma asking the coal man for a bag of coal on tick and she'd pay him next week, I'd go off with me brothers at night, bag the coal on to our backs and off down the train track and she would wake up next morning and the bunker would be full. She often wondered where it came from but daren't ask no questions.

The Christmas after me fifteenth birthday was the first time I let me ma and da know that I was drinking. I told them I was going to a party and that it was a free bar. God I had such a chronic hangover next day! I arrived home at six in the morning, I'd had so much to drink it was coming out of me ears. Me da said he hoped I hadn't been drinking. I said that I was still drunk. I made me ma and da a cup of coffee and went off to bed. I woke up at midday and I walked around town feeling sick every time I walked past a pub; the smell of it! I met me da later

9

that day, he took me into his pub and said, 'If in future you are going to drink I'd rather you do it up-front rather than behind me back so that we can control what you are doing.' I said OK and asked for a Coke. He made me have a real drink. He was good like that. It was like when I started smoking when I was seven, rather than me nicking fags me ma would encourage me to smoke while she was watching and not going OTT [over the top].

In a funny sort of way me mammy and daddy did not encourage us to be kids when we were kids, but when we started growing up we were encouraged to grow up and be responsible. After the Christmas party episode me da took me, Sean and Tom to the pub. He did not know that since I was around nine, I nicked vodka from me home. I liked the taste of it. I used to drink it neat. I liked the taste so much; I even gave it to me baby brother John.

Me da made an arrangement for us to be able to drink in that pub, his local, from then onwards. On occasions me da would drink with us, we'd sit with him and have a few drinks. He'd drink about six or eight pints of Guinness and leave at about eight o'clock. He used to think he was a working man, even when he wasn't working, and that he was entitled to a drink; unfortunately me mammy didn't agree with it. After he'd left, we'd be up the stairs in the pub because we were under age and didn't want to advertise it. I'd drink anything, pints of lager, cider, vodkas. I got to the stage where I was drinking one and a half pints of vodka and I had to be carried home. The barman would be cursing us because we would not let him close the bar. It would be half twelve or one o'clock and we'd still be sitting there!

I got me first ever job when I was fifteen as a trainee general engineer on a government training course. I left that when the course finished six months later. I shouldn't have started it until I was sixteen but I knew someone and I convinced the person who was running it that I should have the job.

I then worked in a butcher's for eighteen months. One day someone came in with a little pup and said if someone didn't take it, it would be put down. I felt sorry for it. So I made up a lot of lies, and convinced me mother that it was a he, that way there would be no pups involved. When they eventually realized that I had lied, I convinced them it was already doctored. So they allowed me to keep her. Me old dog is still in Dublin.

I had to finish that job because I cut me hand on one of the slicing machines cutting rashers. Me hand got infected and I went off sick. After a short while they said that unless I came back to work I would lose me job. Me hand had not healed and so I told them where to put the job.

The first time I ever struck one of me own family was me brother Tom. It was the sorriest moment of me life and it plays on me mind even now. We were having an argument as brothers always do. I was about sixteen, he was fifteen. We were walking together on the top of Jonny (also spelt Johnny) Cullen Hill, we were having a big argument and he said something, turned towards me and I just hit him. It was the sickest moment of me life. He's me brother, me best mate. I just whacked him one. From there I realized what I didn't want to be like. I'd just shown meself I can actually be violent. I hurt him. It probably hurt me more than it did him. It hurt me that I was capable of such a thing. I knew that I had the potential to be violent, but not to me brother. He was me best friend. It wasn't something that I'd deliberately meant for him. He called me a bastard. He fucked off. I think he was crying. We were best friends, even now we are best friends. I speak to him once or twice a week. I still see the look on his face.

Up until I was sixteen, I didn't give a fuck how I looked. As a kid, I was dumpy and ugly. Me ma used to call me an ugly little bastard so I always assumed I was ugly anyway. If I looked at pictures of meself I used to think ugly old swine. I didn't care how I dressed, I used to wear the same clothes for weeks. I never changed – probably to spite me ma and da. But when I started dating girls, I became very conscious of how I looked, how me hair should be and how I should dress.

One night I was over at this girl's house and me ma sent a message over to come home. The girl and I were going through a bad time and that was the last straw, she'd had enough and told me to fuck off. I went off home and got told to wash the dishes, I saw red and I hit her, me

11

mother. I wasn't prepared to take it . Right up to that moment she still used to beat me and pick on me, up until then I couldn't bring meself to hit a woman but now I'd hit one … I've been hit enough times by a woman, and if they are strong enough to hit me I'll do it back. The beatings stopped from that time onwards.

Not long after this, I made it up with the girl and we were due to go around to a ceilidh [Irish dance], me ma was supposed to come round to her house first. She hadn't arrived by about ten o'clock so I went home to find out where she was. She was sitting there crying. Her hair was all over the place. She'd been beaten up. Me da was upstairs in bed. I went up and and dragged him out of bed and then I beat him up. It was a helluva fight which lasted at least an hour. I left the house. I wasn't going to come back. I found somewhere to stay for a few days. When I came back me da was pleased to see me. He brought me into the kitchen and tried to tell me what happens between a husband and wife should not be interfered with. I wouldn't have that. I said if you don't apologize to me ma and get things sorted out I won't come back home. We kids had got to the stage where we didn't want to be listening to it any more. From then on I was encouraging me ma to leave him. We were all virtually grown up and she's been putting up with it for a long time and I'd been putting up with it for nearly as long. Me da was stubborn for a long time but on their wedding anniversary he bought her an engagement ring and apologized to her.

Between times of work I was signing on. I got part-time work with me da, a day here and a day there. I used to sign on and blew me dosh at the fruit machine places. We used to go in and out the factories nicking money. I never bothered about factory names so long as they have an easy roof to get through. We done this place once, a coal yard. We managed to get through the wall where the safe was, but we didn't realize how big the safe was. It was only when we saw it that we realized we had to knock a whole wall down to get at it. When we finally got to the safe we found there was fuck all in it. There should have been because it was coal money collection day. They must have brought in security to pick up the money before we got there.

12

It was coming up to Christmas time, I'd been out on Connaught Street and bought a couple of annuals for me kid brother's Christmas stocking. He still hasn't seen them. I was now back on the dole, cashed me money, done me usual thing, put some in the fruit machine, held on to a few quid for me mother, and held on to a few quid to buy a couple of annuals and a few things for me brother. I'd been talking to a couple of lads and I went off walking down the road and a couple of cops stopped me and told me I'd stolen these annuals. I said that I hadn't and that I'd just got them in the shop. I walked towards the shop and the copper grabbed hold of me and threw me to the ground. So I just got up and laid into him. Both of us ended up covered in blood, then four other cops came along and I got arrested. They done me for stealing the books from someone unknown and charged me with assault. I didn't have a receipt but the girl assistant from behind the counter said she would confirm it. Yet the owners of the bookshop wrote to the court saying they did not sell that particular kind of book. They had probably been told to by the police. I got fined £2 for stealing the book and given a three-month conditional discharge for the assault, that's the way it was in Dublin!

I first had nooky when I was eighteen, in Dublin. This woman was the same age as me mammy – forty-eight. I don't know how it happened. This woman was a manic depressive and I'd been going round, being neighbourly, helping her doing odd jobs for her. She came in one night and she'd gone a bit silly, swallowed a load of pills. She was into killing herself. I had a go at her, made her get sick, then she was whinging and weeping and then the next minute she was all over me. Before I knew it she was on top of me. I was confused. I was lying there praying, 'Get her off'. I had a hard-on but I couldn't come. I didn't feel comfortable. I don't know if it was by consent, I just let her get on with it. I was glad when it was all over. I'd been wanting to have nooky before this with a girl that I'd been going out with, but, when this happened, it near enough put me off sex for life.

Not long after this I was working on the markets and I met this Noelle. She was all right! She had two kids and was the same age as me.

I enjoyed nooky with her. I used to buy condoms, they used to cost £3 for three; but in the heat of the moment never thought to use them. We used to go to parties and used to take whatever pills was going. I didn't know what I was taking half the time. I just used to get out of it. It was a funny situation because we used to stop at two lesbian friends of Noelle's. Me and Noelle would be making it in one bed and the other two would be making it in the other. It was a funny situation as we all used to be watching each other. I wasn't interested in what they were doing, they were obviously happy in what they were doing. It didn't bother me when Noelle got in with them either. I would roll over and fall asleep, I would be knackered. I finished with her when she told me she was pregnant. I couldn't be doing with that. She started going out with me mate who done the markets with me. She had the kid afterwards – it could have been mine, it could have been anybody's the way the relationship was going.

The parties were the best, I'd be off at three in the morning, me ma thought I was off to get ready for the markets. I used to take hash, Valium, temazepam, just popping pills to get a buzz. I used to be so off me face at the Saturday morning markets. I made a fortune selling stuff. I sold anything that people would buy: watches, biscuits and washing-up liquid. We'd go to the market places and buy the stuff in bulk, dirt cheap. We'd do door to door during the week and at the weekends we'd do the markets. We always went to parties before the markets. I used to sit there so full of confidence. One time I thought I was flying and went over towards a whole load of potatoes and I ended up flying all over them!

We were always being harassed by the cops. I was standing on the edge of a pavement, there was me, a couple of me brothers and a couple of friends outside Jack Dolan's warehouse. The cops went whizzing by and then the next minute they were back, rode the car on to the footpath and then hit me on the knee. I said, 'You fucking eejit!' He said, 'Who are you calling a fucking eejit?' He then said, 'Here, come on.' We knew once they took their belt off and the hat, we could fight with them; and so I laid into him. Me brothers and friends were standing back making sure everything was OK, in case any other cops came. Then another car arrived. Another cop came across and I went BANG and hit him. I left three of the cops in a bit of a mess! Me brothers told me to back off now. A cop managed to handcuff one of me hands. I wrapped meself around the lamppost so they couldn't move me but they managed to get me in the car.

We went back to the cop shop and they left me in a cell to cool down. Me da came down, me brothers had already told him it wasn't me fault. They took me to court next morning, the case went on for a long time. I was working at the time and they went up as character witnesses which was really good. The court did not take into account when I got done for the annuals, I had a three-month suspended and three years' bind over to keep the peace.

One of the main reasons I came to London was being hooked on the machines. I thought I was never going to get off them unless I got out of Dublin. They were doing me head in. It felt like it was exploding. There had been a couple of lads who had committed suicide. The machines are a bastard thing when you get involved with them. If I had a pound, I would walk a mile and a half into town just to play the pound. The government tried bringing in this law to help people – you should only make a 2p bet each time at the most. The places exploited that: you could lay as much as you liked, win as much as you liked but if the cops walked through the door the owners could flick a switch and turn on the machines back to the original 2p bet. Nobody ever won on that.

There were different laws for different parts of the town. The tourists could carry on gambling all the time, a load of old women could gamble away for the whole weekend. It's like a Mafia-controlled thing, it's big business: everybody's got a lot of money on them. I used to think someone should burn the fuckers down. There were no advice places for people to go and get help except Gamblers Anonymous, which I went to on a couple of occasions, but then I'd go from there straight into the fruit machine places. I tried and tried to come off them but I couldn't. When I was signing on the dole the only responsibility was to give me ma half the money; I wasn't even capable of doing that. I was getting the money and blowing it all on the poker machines. I was trying to beat the computer all the time.

Me ma would give me money to pay the rent and I would go straight past the rent office into the amusement arcade. Playing the machine, back to the cash counter again, blowing your balls, not caring. Before I'd go home I'd have the money back, I may not have paid the rent, but I had the money. Once or twice I slipped up and I'd not been able to get the money back and I'd get the living daylights kicked out of me. I became very bad on the machines, I got to the stage that I got suicidal on them.

I used to lose everything; me dole or me wages, straight on them machines every week. I was getting to the stage when I was just breaking in and out of factories and shops to get the money. The dole office was in the middle of town and of course in the middle of town there was about twenty fruit machine places and poker machine places. Even if I went in to play a fruit machine or a poker machine I'd be in playing the space invaders and everything else – getting more addicted to everything. Anything that was taking me money and giving me two minutes' pleasure or giving me a chance to forget for those two minutes; playing the poker machine I was in another world.

In March '88, the day I came over here to England, I collected me dole money, did me usual thing and went to the poker machine and blew it. Then I went on a bit of a spree stealing, and returned money that I'd borrowed. I said, 'That's it, I've had enough! I can either carry on doing this and get meself into more trouble with the family or I can come over to England and start from scratch.' So I got the money together. I didn't say cheerio to anyone. Me ma thought I'd just been up to collect the dole money, she'd assume that I'd blown me money again and so I'd be hiding out in Dublin. The last person I saw and said cheerio to was the guy who drove the bus. He knew us so well he would stop the bus anywhere in the road to let us on. He never charged me any fare. He was a decent guy and gave me a couple of English pounds. If me ma had seen him she would have known that I was off to get some work and get meself sorted out from those poxy poker machines.

I had only enough money to get a child's ticket for the boat and train. I was small enough and could pass for a child. I was very thin and only five foot three, even though I was eighteen; I looked very baby-faced. No one questioned it even when the guy came up to me on the train, I thought they were going to pull me. All I could think about was that I was starving and I had more or less admitted to meself that it was not going to be easy. I kept looking out the window and thinking that was something I'd never seen before.

I got the train from Holyhead to Euston. I arrived at some time in the evening and what was going through me mind was that I didn't even have a penny. I had 3p in Irish money. Me youngest brother was already in London. He'd arranged everything before he came over, someone in Dublin had got him a job in a pub. He left because of me ma, the way she picked on him too, and he thought nobody liked him. I knew me brother was in Clapham but I thought he was in *Clapton*. I didn't have the price of a tube fare, it was a different country so I didn't know about dodging fares, I only learned to do that afterwards. I asked someone the directions to Clapton. I walked all the way there.

I checked all the pubs, it was freezing cold, I searched high and low, every pub in the place. I didn't have a heavy jacket or anything. I didn't bring anything with me, just the clothes I stood up in. I thought he must be here somewhere, I might have missed a few pubs. Then they were all closed and I had to wait till morning. I found a school where they had been doing some work on it and I got in and just started to settle and then I saw two rottweilers. I was straight over the wall then. I wasn't going to be stopping there! So I just wandered around till the pubs opened again in the morning. I'd spent all night wandering around and I was totally pissed off.

I was starving and I knew I'd bought a one-way ticket and there was no turning back. I knew I was in a situation that I wasn't going to have a roof over me head and I had no money for food. The only people who could tell me where to go were those living on the streets or winos or dossers. So I went back to the Euston station, I'd seen some of them back there the night before.

At the back of the station I heard them talking about 'Simon's'. They said they were going there later this evening, 'you can follow us'. They were friendly and I met them later. I was hallucinating, so cold, so tired, I hadn't had any sleep for two nights. I got to the Simon Community [a community of homeless people and volunteers living and working with London's street homeless] and they weren't going to let me in. I told them me age and what the score was and why I was here. I looked so tiny. All I was concerned about was someone giving me something to eat. Fuck the sleep. They took me to a little room and gave me the most beautiful bowl of soup I've ever had and a beautiful slice of bread. They offered me more but I had so much hunger inside me; I'd devoured the soup in seconds and made a glutton of meself, that I wasn't able to eat any more. I had a nice bed, a shower, and I felt more positive about things in the morning.

They said that I would have to go to Centrepoint [centre providing accommodation for young homeless people] tomorrow night. I hadn't a clue what Centrepoint was. They rang them in advance to refer me, drew me a map and gave me a ticket to get there. One of the lads took me up to make sure I didn't get lost. I was quite happy to stay there and get meself sorted out.

I stayed at Centrepoint's Dean Street emergency night shelter. They asked me why I was here. Was I on the run? It was all right. The boys and girls who were there at the time were just ordinary people who were in the same position I was in. They were nice people but I thought a bit weird to start off with. When we started talking to each other, everyone realized we were in a similar position. I stayed there on and off for about three weeks.

What I was intending to do was use that as a base and try and find me brother and a job and get meself somewhere to live sorted out. The basic things they told me when they were trying to sort me out was we can give you X amount of days, then you must sign on. I couldn't sign on because I had no identification. I had to go to the Soho Project [advice centre for homeless people in the West End], they referred me to the Irish Centre [front-line welfare advice and advocacy for Irish immigrants], who gave me the money for a birth certificate, which was an English one. Both helped me try to sort out me benefits and housing.

I had an argument at Centrepoint because you had to be in at eight in the evening and out at eight in the morning. You could get pneumonia in an hour out there. I told them you don't turn up on the streets with a suitcase, you turn up in whatever you've got. Me objection was that eight o'clock was not a suitable time to be allowing people to be let in. If you turned up later they would not let you in. So you must turn up at eight. Restrictions and curfews – you might as well be back at home. Then we'd be kicked out at eight in the morning and it was freezing cold then as well.

I ended up in a bit of a situation because I couldn't get the dole because I didn't have any ID [official identification such as a birth certificate] and could only spend up to three days in various hostels. It took them some time to get me ID sorted, and I ended up on the streets and in the nick for highway obstruction before it got sorted. Me probation couldn't even sort that one out. Between the Soho Project and the Irish Centre they referred me to St George's hostel for young offenders; no one else would have me. It was a very nice hostel, and then they said they couldn't have me because me previous record was too violent. I couldn't win, so I went off to join the lads down at the Embankment.

It was all right stopping down at the Embankment, down at the bridge on Villiers Street. There were always fires going and there were always plenty of blankets. Charities, and all sorts of weirdos preaching at you, were always coming down with a bowl of soup, bread, sandwiches and blankets. I was with a girl, Rachael, a Scottish girl who I'd met in Centrepoint. There was a gang of us young ones and we all used to look after each other. It was a bit of a dodgy place under the arches. I didn't exactly live in a cardboard box; you would put cardboard underneath to stop the cold and then cover yourself with the blankets.

In the daytime, our gang went begging on Hungerford Bridge. We would take it in turns, Peter would get up first and play his mouth organ, Mick and Jim would go up and do a bit of tap dancing, me and Rachael they would be sorry for us; with our size, we'd just sit there, a couple trying to make it in the world. We could make £55 in an hour from the tourists and commuters.

Normally it would be at night-time when everyone else was asleep we had nooky because it was companionship, something to be doing. A few drinks, you didn't give a fuck whether there was someone watching or not. Your heads under the blankets, they'd see this little butt go up and down.

When me and Rachael got the crabs, we didn't know. Living on the streets, you could have anything. You wouldn't take much notice to what was going on. We were inside St James's Park in these bushes, and we were doing a bit of nooky, it was in the middle of the day. For the first time since I'd been going out with her, I'd seen her crotch. I went fucking hell! What's that? She was crawling! I just thought, what the fuck is that! Her whole pubes was just matted with crabs. Her fanny was matted with them, totally matted! She didn't know. I looked at meself, we realized that there was something there, boy. Jeez, I was nearly sick. I said, we've got to speak to somebody. I'd been going with her for about a month, I thought I haven't felt any itching. I'll tell you, we wouldn't have; although we washed every day at the Passage [day centre, based in Victoria, providing a wide range of support for homeless people] we were still dirty, living in the dirt, you'd get used to an itch and you wouldn't pay it any attention. You just accepted it. You'd made your mind up not to think about it. We scratched our way to the Passage.

We had to wash our hair out, with this stuff. They put special stuff in with our clothes to wash them. They had to disinfect everything. I was too embarrassed to see the doctor. So there was this clinic kind of a woman, a specific medical nun. We saw her and we went straight into this pure white room; just the two showers and we had to wash each other, to make sure you get it everywhere, backs, necks, ears, behind the ears, the hair, everything. It was probably the best wash I ever had in me life!

I got paid me dole money about six weeks after I got to London. Rachael and I got paid in Whitechapel and made a friend there, Ziggy. He was a bit of a nutter and looked like John Lennon. We'd been in the pub, had a few bevvies, then walking down Wardour Street these three guys started on us. I'd been given a knife earlier in the day to hold for somebody, a lock knife, which I kept open. Ziggy was carrying a scalpel. There was me, Ziggy and Rachael. These three blokes thought, *a zoo walking up the road*, they said something to Ziggy, he pulled out the scalpel. I jumped between him and the guy as he was going to cut the guy up. Another guy grabbed hold of me, he was about sixteen stone and I was about eight stone, and he threw me straight on the road. I came back and started laying into him and punched his head in. Ziggy had slashed his man right across the neck, he needed seventy stitches. Before we knew it, the cops were coming from all sides. The cops grabbed me as the knife flew into a taxi. They arrested us. I got charged with ABH [actual bodily harm] or something and couldn't get bail because I was NFA [of no fixed abode]. I spent three weeks in custody in Feltham and, after they sentenced me, the final week in Hollesley Bay [both young offender institutions].

When I was in Feltham it was like being in a hotel. It was a break from lying on a bit of cardboard, anyway. I was in a single room, locked up for twenty-three hours in a day. I used to talk to the black guy in the cell next to me. There was a hole in the wall and we used to slide joints through. We sat there merrily stoned and chatting. They'd give you a comb and 'sandpaper' to wipe your arse with, and when I was really pissed off I'd wrap that around the comb and make a bit of music. After I was released I was back down the Embankment with Rachael.

I used to get too drunk and wake up in the gutter, or in the cop shop; I was only sometimes charged with disorderly conduct. Usually, I was just locked up for the night to sober up and have some breakfast in the morning. On the other mornings there was a ritual. We used to be up at seven every morning and straight up the Passage for breakfast. You could get it free if you went to the nun and you'd get a ticket, but it used to cost next to nothing anyway. For 25p you'd have a decent enough meal. For 15p you'd get a bag of washing done, it used to be dirt cheap for everything. You'd get a razor, a bit of soap and a shower for 10p. It was clean enough; it was very clean. You'd leave there and then you could go back in there and have another sleep, crash out on the comfy chairs or have a chat with everybody else.

I didn't miss Ireland, I spent most of me time out of me face. I wasn't really interested. I had to make sure at the end of the day I had a bite to eat, a blanket to put over me head and me next bottle of Thunderbird, Valium and anything else to get out of your brain. I'd lost interest in 'ordinary' people and 'everyday' living. As far as I was concerned, people were there to be begged off.

Rachael got pregnant, it could have been anybody's. The council gave us bed and breakfast accommodation in Pimlico. We stayed in bed all day and then we went begging. We cut out the monster drinking and only bought the odd drink. We had cooking facilities in the room and so when we were getting money we just whacked it on food. Given the opportunity, I would have sorted meself out at that time, but Rachel ended up in hospital and lost the baby. I was very upset. We then lost the bed and breakfast as she was no longer pregnant and she went off with one of me best mates. The relationship lasted three months.

When we'd finished, I started hanging out with, and then moved in with, a few young guys who were living in a squat in Peckham Park Road. We had no money and so we went out to rob or mug people. We mugged a few people but it was something I didn't like to be doing. One of the guys decided he was going out on the game and said that he was off to do a punter and get some money. I thought, well if he can do it, so can I. I think maybe he'd done it before.

We got very drunk and I asked him questions about what I should do. I was told to always use a condom and charge £50. We went to Piccadilly and the next moment I thought what the fuck's happened to him, where's he gone? Next thing I got me first punter and he drove back to his place. I had no idea where he lived. I was drunk and I wasn't bothered. Nice guy, I got to know him over the years afterwards. I fucked him with a condom, got me money and then he drove me to the Golden Lion pub afterwards and I got blind drunk.

I started hanging around with other people on the Dilly [Piccadilly] and doing punters regularly, spending all me money getting blind drunk.

I hoped that whoever picked me up wasn't a copper. There's always the JPUs [the police juvenile protection unit] hanging around, you've got to be stupid to go over to them. They were always around your age, they wouldn't be hanging around with the punters. I've never been arrested on the Dilly. During me time there, we had a source from the cop shop, so we always knew when a raid was going on. We'd be hiding behind Eros when the raid started.

I didn't stay on the Dilly long. I spent most of me time in the Golden Lion, it was much safer doing business there and I could get drunk, and they had a machine. When the money ran out, which was every night, I was spending £150 a day on drinking and the machine. When you are standing around in the pub you are inclined to get a bit bored and I'd put a penny or two in the machine and they'd all add up. I did about three punters a day. I still go out every now and again and spend £200 or £300 a night.

I didn't mind doing the rent, it's nothing I'm ashamed of. As far as I was concerned it was a way of survival. I didn't mind having to do the sex, I just blanked it out in me head. That's what I've been doing all me life anyway. The guy who introduced me to it was straight, a lot of rent boys are straight, you just adapt your brain. I was still going out with girls.

This scene became me life. The first punter I ever done introduced me to Terry. He kept saying to Terry, what you need is a good fuck. Terry met me with him and asked me if I would like to go back to his place. He said I could go back to his flat and drink as much as I liked. We sat up the whole night talking, that was a Friday night. Next morning he hadn't been anywhere near me, all we had done was talking, then he took me shopping. For some peculiar reason we got on really well from the start. That's all we done, talked. Then we sat down later that day drinking and talking. It turned out we liked each other. We became best friends. Terry was in love with me. He had too much respect for me to touch me. We never had sex. We'd be in the same bed together but he would be off on the other side. He was a good friend. He committed suicide two years ago almost to the day.

Some punters became long-term friends. At first they'd see me for sex, then they'd like me personality and then they'd want to look after me. I could and still can ring them up at any time and they'd help me out with no strings attached. They fell in love with me.

In August '88 I was in the Golden Lion and I met this guy David, he wasn't a punter. For some peculiar reason I liked him. He liked me from the minute he first saw me, it was love at first sight. People have hang-ups about guys going with guys; as far as I've been concerned all me life, sex is sex. It's what two men may have, what two women may have or a man and a woman may have. Sex is dipping your wick into a hole and making it come. That's the basic fact around it. Whether it's a man's hole or a woman's hole – sex is sex.

David sent a friend over to ask me out. Apart from the rent, I had never been with a guy before, I wasn't sure what was the score. Then he came over and asked me out. I liked his bottle – the nerve. So I went out to dinner with him, on a Thursday. We had goodness how many bottles of wine. I don't think he wanted to leave me in the state I was in, and so he took me home with him. I don't even remember getting back to his place.

We didn't have sex that night, we were a bit wary of it, but when I woke up next morning, he was kneeling over me with his cock in me mouth. I went errrrr … I actually enjoyed it. I was a bit surprised. The following morning, I left. He dropped me down at the station and he said he'd like to see me again. I thought well, it was all right. I was a little bit embarrassed about it. I thought I'll ring him. I'd got a good vibe about him right from the start.

I'd been to Brighton the following weekend with a girlfriend. While I was away David phoned me at the squat. I rang him back. I arranged to meet him in town. We had a couple of drinks and he then left for the Piano Bar. I went off and got a burger. I knew that he had another half, Tony, and I felt a bit guilty about that. But I liked him so much I thought I'd go and find him. He was sat there with Tony. I kept calling David over saying, come and talk to me. I liked the look of him, I was attracted to him, I felt comfortable around him, the whole works.

24

Nothing more happened that night. I was really feeling for him. I started following him about. I was fanatical about him. I started hounding him; I'd go to the club where he was working. He was happy to let it be a bit on the side, but I wanted to go out with him. It was going on like this for a while. I wasn't going back with him and having sex, just following him about and kissing him from time to time.

He came over to the squat one night, he took one look around the place and said he didn't like where I was stopping; it was disgusting. 'You can't stop here', he said. 'Come in and move in with me.' I said, 'OK, but you've got to get rid of Tony, I'm not playing second fiddle.' He did, he got rid of him.

The reason why we took the HIV test was because me and David had been going out a while and we were uncomfortable. We wanted to have fun with each other, to enjoy it. We didn't want to stop half-way through and put a condom on. It was inconvenient and they hurt me. It's a bit embarrassing standing there and the condom is too tight, it chokes the top of your willy, and then you lose it and then you have to try again. We wanted to have an ordinary sexual relationship which was not uncomfortable, irritating; condoms were irritating for me. We wanted to have a special relationship without the need of a big chunk of rubber stuck in the way. The two of us liked each other that much. People would argue that the benefits of wearing it are a lot more. I thought about them, but I wanted to feel the benefits of his flesh against me flesh. It was the meaning of love and closeness. So for our own benefit, we thought we'd have a test.

Me result came back positive. I was HIV-positive. David's negative.

What more could happen to me in me life? I was just nineteen, and I found meself in an environment where I was happy for the first time in me life. Echoes of 'I'll make you regret the day you were ever born' came flooding back. I believed me ma had put a curse on me.

I felt me head was exploding, I was frightened to death. I started getting blind drunk every night. Then I started fitting with the alcohol. When I fitted, I never knew where I was, I got out of control and violent with it. I was told I was epileptic, but I still had to have the drink.

25

I started beating David up when I was completely out of it; he thought I was going to kill him. I found knives under the bed, and asked him why they were there. He said that it was in case of burglars. It hit me then, just how I'd become; that really shook me. I was fighting on the street and the police were always picking me up.

I was desperate and so very frightened. I started overdosing whenever I could lay me hands on any pills. Then I started doing me wrists. I was told by David that one day, I pulled him into the bathroom, locked him in there, and hacked at me wrists, there, right in front of him, screaming for help.

David and his friends were continuously taking me to the different local hospitals. I got admitted to one, only to be told two weeks later that there was nothing wrong with me! Jeez, me head was exploding so much, and they tell me there's nothing wrong. I was totally fucked up.

David's health was getting bad, he was having to take the Valiums. He was getting to be unable to cope with me. He had a job and was working all hours, he had to look after me, and the flat which I kept smashing up.

He took me to another hospital and signed the papers saying that I was a danger to meself and to others. Me lover had sectioned me. I needed him so much, how could he do this to me? I thought he wanted rid of me. They kept me in there and told me I'd got a personality disorder. That's clever! Now I'd got meself a psychiatric illness as well. I thought I was going mad.

When I got discharged I was so mad, I went down to David's work with me section papers and started to smash the place up. I was wild, I wanted to know why he'd put me there. He got suspended from his job because of me. But I wanted him to meself at home.

I couldn't figure out where I could have got the HIV. I'd always used a condom on the rent and they'd never broken. The only other guy I'd been with was David, and I only used to do blow jobs. We never actually fucked, and he was HIV-negative. From me knowledge of how the infection is passed on it had to come from Rachael, but I never actually believed you could get it from a female.

She was a smack user, injecting. She never jacked up in front of me. She used to piss off with all her mates and then I'd meet her and she would be completely flying out of it and I wouldn't know what she had been taking or doing. You could join the dots on her arms. I never injected.

Rachael and I didn't use condoms because we were too out of our heads. There was no messages about safer sex out there on the streets and no condoms. I don't think people expected you to be having sex, while living rough. Which is a thing they tend to forget. I went and found her on the streets, and she told me she was HIV-positive.

David decided to have me move out of the flat. He said I would have to learn to be taking responsibility for meself, because I'd got so dependent on him. He said it would be good for me to see me old street friends. The council housed me because of our circumstances. Then David went away to America. He ended up there a year. He was making himself ill here and had already started to see a psychiatrist himself. Me violence had brought up his childhood violence. I was missing David, so frightened and alone.

I went back on the rent to pay for me drink and to find me friends. I started going back to the Soho Project. Then one of me old friends, who'd been doing the rent from the squat days, took me to Streetwise. I went up there a lot and was now ready in talking about the HIV. Once I'd started talking to people about it, I started to have some better days; some which weren't as bad as others. I started to talk about me childhood and saw that me exploding head and anger and being frightened had always been there anyway, it was just a whole lot worse now. Things kept going wrong with me health and they took me to the clinic.

I got in touch with me da on the phone at his local pub and then started phoning him regular. I got John, me younger brother's, address here and we started seeing each other. I went back to Ireland for Christmas and told them about me HIV. No one believed it. But they were kind, except me ma, all she was interested in was how much benefits I was getting and wanting money from me. I went back to Ireland several times, she was just the same. I took David over there a couple of times, they were OK about me being gay. The family never spoke about the

HIV. I was still close to me brothers and sister and I liked to see them. I realized now I'd grown up, what a bastard me ma was. I was always ill with the stress when I went over there.

I made a lot of friends, many were me old punters, some rich and kind. One helped me get me portfolio together and I was taken on by a photographic modelling agency. It was all above board, no sleaze, but I couldn't accept any work because I was too ashamed of me body. People told me I had real good looks but I could never see them.

I spent time doing odd jobs for friends, helping with painting and decorating. They'd gave me easy jobs to do and then they'd pay me a lot of money, it was their way of helping me out. I did the odd car boot sale from time to time.

I got rehoused because me bedsit was too small. With me drenching night sweats and diarrhoea, I needed more space, a place better for me deteriorating health. I got a one-bedroom flat, and after David got back from America he moved in with me. He is and was the only man for me. He cares for me.

February, last year, I got admitted to hospital for tests. I still had me exploding head and a lot of pains. The hospital never knew quite what it was. I was treated for pneumonia but I never really got better. I got me AIDS diagnosis. I was in shock. I kept going back, but tests never showed anything. Was it all in me head?

A lot of people knew me health problems in the West End because I've never lied to them. People always come up and ask me things and talk to me about their problems anyway and I'm easy to talk to. I'd give them condoms. After me time in hospital, Streetwise trained me to do the clubs and bars; to talk to other rent boys of the dangers and problems out there, to give them advance information using what I had learnt from mine and other people's problems.

I was still getting blinding headaches, night sweats and huge temperatures at night. I knew something was not right. But all the time tests kept showing nothing was wrong. I was readmitted to the hospital and discharged home at Christmas; still unable to find anything wrong. David could see everything was wrong. He told me later that I didn't know where I was or anything. He was panicking. I wasn't holding down me food or anything. I was down to seven stone in weight. Through David's contacts, I was admitted to another hospital within the next week. They diagnosed me brain tumour two days later. Life has finally done me head in.

Indeed, me ma has won. Me ma has finally made me regret the day I was born. I must have been some evil, evil bastard to have to go through the hell I'm going through.

RIP: Madser died six weeks later with David, his mother, father, family and friends around him.

'Jason/Zoe'

I had my sex change operation six weeks ago: now my whole body looks just like a woman's. Inside, I feel very female: just like a woman. I will never be a 'real' woman: at the end of the day I'm transsexual. I had to get it right into my head, as soon as I knew I was transsexual, that I will never be child-bearing or tuna-smelling.

I was a pre-cum baby. My dad pulled out before he came, to make sure my mum wouldn't get pregnant. I never got the full whack. I've got three older sisters. My mum had three miscarriages before I came along: they were all boys. She couldn't carry boys, and so they hadn't planned to have any more children. So when I came along, a baby boy, twenty-two years ago, everyone was overjoyed.

I grew up in North Wales. I had a wonderful upbringing in my family. My mother is the most caring woman in the world, full of love and affection. The best in the world. Ever since I can remember, my mum has always been there for me. We've been so close from a very early age. We'd talk about all sorts of things. My mum says to me now that there was something not quite right with me from a very early age. She knew something was wrong. My mother, my wonderful, wonderful mother, for as long as I can remember, she was a really good mother. She did everything for her children. We could talk about our problems. Me and her especially, were really close. I used to cry a lot. If I'd had a nightmare or people had been calling me names that day at school, she'd just come into my room and we'd talk. It's just a big, wonderful story about how wonderful she was and still is!

My sisters are fabulous. I've always got on really well with them. If I got hassle at school, all my sisters would stick up for me. I was always their little brother. They were always very loving and protective. Jean, my sister, who was closest to me in age, we would fight all the time, but we were still best friends.

My dad had a shop. He is a very successful, self-made businessman. A typical hard-working man, he always provided a lot for us; we never went hungry. My parents have a happy marriage.

For a long time he was very jealous of me and my mum's relationship. I used to take my mother's side in their arguments. I think it hurt him that I was closer to my mum. With her, I could be the little girl inside. I was doing everything with mummy. I wasn't the little boy my dad could play football with, or take out. I was never like that. So I think he felt rejected. When I was growing up we never really spoke, we never really communicated. I wouldn't sit down and talk about my feelings with him. He was a man's man and we didn't have anything in common. He was a little bit hard but very soft. He is a good father. We are a close-knit family. There was no sort of hatred in the family. We were brought up to be kind. We did a lot of things as a family.

We used to go to the beach, have picnics in the fields, go horse-riding and play with the dolls. We used to get the dolls out and dress them up. When I was very, very little, by the age of three, I used to really love dolls. One day, my dad brought this doll home. It was one that cried and wet its nappy. My sisters were going, 'I want it', and I was screaming, 'I want it!' I screamed until I was blue in the face; I had to have that bloody doll. In the end, my dad gave it to me.

When we were really young we went to swimming lessons twice a week on Tuesdays and Thursdays. I started karate at six: I got my purple belt. Then my sisters dropped out and so did I. I've never used my karate since.

I used to really look like a girl when I was little. I used to have a crew cut, so people wouldn't compare me to a girl. Yet still everyone used to mistake me for a girl. It was very upsetting at the time. Everyone was coming up to my mum saying what a beautiful girl you have. My

31

mother used to whisper to them that I was a boy. They would say that I was too pretty to be a boy. I was listening to these things going on above my head. My god, I had my identity crisis from four years old.

I would overhear some of my sisters' boyfriends saying to them, 'Is that your sister?' about me. More often than not, my sisters went, 'Yes'. They didn't have the heart to say, 'No, he's my brother'. I used to get really upset about it. How embarrassing. It was horrible. I used to cry at night, I didn't understand it.

Growing up at school was a nightmare. People say it was the best years of their life: they'd love to go back and do it all again. I'll tell you something now, honey: I'd rather be hanged. I would have loved school if I'd gone as a girl.

I started school at the age of three. I remember my first day: I didn't want to go. My mum handed me over to the teacher. I was kicking and screaming. My mum, she was so wonderful, she came back a couple of hours later to see if I was OK. I was playing in the sandpit. I always remember when I was little, making the castles. I found the sandpit so soothing. I used to love it.

I was very much a loner, always have been. I didn't really play with the other kids; although sometimes I hung around with the girls. I never felt right. It could have been a lack of confidence.

I hated football: anything that boys did I couldn't stand. I was used to playing with my dolls. I didn't enjoy being with the boys. They were aggressive, clumsy monsters. Little school was the worst. The trauma of endlessly getting called names, because I was so girly, was a nightmare. The kids were so cruel.

They'd be calling me names like 'poofter', 'pansy' all the time. They said, you look like a girl, you talk like a girl. I was so feminine when I was little: I hated it.

The worst thing was that the school playground was right across the street from our house. My mum could see me, and when I got home, she used to say, how come you are never playing football in the big field at playtime? I was too embarrassed. I often used to hang around on my own. I didn't enjoy little school.

I was six years old when I started to fantasize about men. I used to think about sex and men. Some people say to me that that is impossible. I used to dream that I was this beautiful girl and I'd always have a boyfriend. It was around this time I had my first orgasm. I woke up in the wet sheets: and then I discovered the way to do it. I remember walking around for about six months thinking that I was the only person who knew how to do this. I really thought that if men knew how to masturbate, they wouldn't need to be unfaithful to their wives. I thought I'd discovered the biggest secret in the world. I didn't know that every fucker was doing it as well.

When I was ten, I remember being in the public toilet and I saw all these holes in the wall. Surprise, surprise! I started looking through them and I saw these men getting off together. I could see these men masturbating. I was trembling. I thought, oh my god! I knew I wanted to do something. I had these sexual feelings and so I left my cubicle door open and someone came in. He fondled me down there, while he masturbated himself. He asked me to suck him. I looked at it; it was all horrible and purple. I couldn't do it. It was all over when he came two minutes later. He slipped a £5 note into my hand.

As soon as I came out of the toilet I burst into tears. What have I done? I thought: *my first sexual realization.* I went straight back to my dad's shop. My sister was at the counter and I blurted out that this man had interfered with me. The police were called in, and for weeks I'd be sitting with this police guy outside the toilets, looking to see if I could see the man. I saw him a few times but I didn't tell them; because after I'd had time to calm down, and to analyse it, I realized how, with what I knew now, I could get a big fat purse.

Even though I was ten years old, I sort of knew what I'd done and that I'd encouraged it. It wasn't a man forcing me to do things: it was him wanting it, and me saying OK. For me, I don't think it was abuse. I let it go on and I wanted it to happen. But, looking back now, I think from the man in the toilet's point of view, he should have known better. He should have thought, *this kid is too young.* He didn't want a homosexual thing: he wanted someone very young and naive. So I think what he did

33

was wrong. He was a paedophile. OK, I could handle it: but what if it was another ten-year-old that didn't know what was going on? Those circumstances meant a lot of kids could have been really fucked up by that: but not little old me. It was the start of a great career as a prostitute.

A year later, when I was eleven, and things had calmed down, I went back to the toilets to make money. At weekends, I used to do the rounds of the toilets; in Rhyl, Colwyn Bay, all of them places. During the week, I'd say to my mother that I was just going over the road to my friend's, to do my homework. The school was there as well. I used to get the punters to park in the school car park and I would do french [oral sex] with them in their cars. I got a couple of regulars; one of them gave me £15 twice a week, and one paid me £20. Men used to come into the toilets and I used to get between £5 and £20 for each. By the time I was thirteen I'd get about £100 a week. In addition, my father, when he used to come in drunk, after Friday night out with the lads, used to give me a tenner, to take my girlfriend out! I used to have all this money.

It was having all this money that got me through big school. Instead of people calling me names, I was the most popular kid in school because I had all this money. Anyone who wanted a pound or two used to come to me. It controlled things that way. They all knew my father had money; so they just assumed that I was getting it off him.

My mum and I were always very close. But between the ages of eleven and thirteen was a time of me continuously shutting her out, and answering her back. Basically I was a real brat. Our close bond went for a while because I did not want to express myself to her or tell her what was going on. It was through no fault of hers. I think in general most kids go through that. I would just say it was just general adolescent hormones taking their effect and were making me unhappy. What with school and everything else, my mother ended up being the person I could take it out on.

I've now sort of told my mum about my times down the toilets. She was devastated. I shouldn't really have told her. She sat there and cried. She really blames herself. She thinks she was a bad mother. She thought she was always there for me. I was given a lot of trust. I was allowed out and to cross the road on my own. I was a responsible child. Wales wasn't like London, with kids being abducted. She doesn't really like hearing about the toilets. She feels really terrible. Even now she feels bad as she knows that this was linked to me being a prostitute.

At thirteen, I wanted to run away and be the most expensive whore in town. I thought, I can go to London. I knew what I wanted. I was qualified to do fuck all. I hated taking orders. I had my own way of thinking about things. I knew that it was a route into success. Looking back now, sometimes I think I wish I'd stayed on at school and got some qualifications.

I used to skip all the time from big school. You couldn't do it in the little school because they'd know. From the age of eleven onwards, I skipped loads of lessons. In the beginning I just skipped PE. I just couldn't stand it. I hated it. I would refuse to play football, bloody rugby and cricket. I loathed sports like that. I had nothing in common with a whole gang of boys. They were all talking about things which I got bored with. That's why I truanted. I used to look over at the girls playing rounders and thought, I want to play rounders.

Later, I started truanting more and more. I would not agree to do the Welsh classes, even though they put me in the first grade – the best class. It was too difficult for me. I didn't like it. They insisted I should be in it because I did well in the exams. It was getting me down because Welsh is such a complicated language, and I just didn't enjoy it.

When I first truanted, I used to go to the doctor. I used to sit in the doctor's surgery and make up some excuse to the doctor because I had stomach acid. Every week, at least once a week, I went to the doctors. Sometimes I used to sit there, and then leave not bothering seeing him. Other times I would sit in the toilets in school, until the lesson was over. Or I just went off somewhere during break and then skipped off afterwards. I went to the fields, cafés, anything. Usually I skipped off on my own. If you skip off with someone else you usually get caught.

Subjects I liked at school were art, music, history. I really enjoyed English, reading, writing too: probably because I was the best in the class at these. I wanted to do cookery as well but couldn't, because of pressure. When you get to choose your own subjects, I didn't have the guts to take cookery and needlework. I knew it would give me so much flak. I did metalwork and woodwork instead. I loathed it. I used to pay people a couple of quid to make a little boat or whatever. I was useless. When my heart's not into something, I just can't do it. The girls made these fabulous soufflés and whatever, and there was me with my bloody metalwork and woodwork.

I was good at school, but when it came to exams, I hated studying. My mind used to drift all the time. I always got good grades. I was always Bs, I was never Ds or Es. I never had the will to have A grades, although I think I could have. I think if I'd gone to school as a girl I would have done fabulously. School was somewhere I had to go and I couldn't wait until 3.30 when it was finished. I was never happy; I was so withdrawn. The teachers never bothered if you had a problem. It wasn't a very nice school, actually. A bit old-fashioned. Built in the 1600s and with the same principle values. I have no fond memories. I shut out the bad times. I sort of drifted through it. I couldn't wait to leave.

I'd love to have gone into art or cookery or law. There was lots of things I wanted to do. I regret in a little way not going the full hog, like going to college, university. I could have got a really good job and made lots of money that way. I feel cheated that way. I don't think I've got the energy to go back to school now: too much like hard work.

My mother used to always make us be self-sufficient. For as long as I can remember she was telling us what was what. We used to clean our own rooms. She taught us all how to cook. When I was thirteen, I could do a Sunday dinner. I was a better cook then than I am now. Now, I can't be bothered. I'm a very plain kind of a cook. It's an ambition of mine to go to night school and learn how to do the different cuisines. Starting off mainly with English and then going on to different nationalities, to be a really great cook. It's the only way to a man's heart: through his balls and through his stomach, especially as they get older.

My parents had ambitions for me. My mother used to build me up and say you are going to do great things. She used to take an interest in my schoolwork and anything else. My father's idea was for me to go into the family business. I really wanted to be a lawyer at one time. When I was very young I was going to be a doctor. If I'd known then what I know now, about the twenty or thirty grand they make a week, I should have been a plastic surgeon.

Me and my mum often used to come up to London when I was thirteen and fourteen. We'd come up for the week or so. We used to stay in the Euston Square Hotel, Euston. We had separate rooms. Because I was doing all this whoring I had loads of money. I remember the first time we went up, we were on Oxford Street and my mother was going into C&A. I said to her that I wanted to go into Top Shop. She said that it was just up the road. Jokingly she said, 'Whatever you do *don't* go into Soho.' So of course, as soon as I was out of her sight, '*Taxi!*' I went to Soho.

I was walking around Soho, and these girls propositioned me. I said, 'No thanks, you're not what I want.' I'd accepted being gay by then. I thought I was gay: I knew I liked men. I carried on walking around and when I was stood on Old Compton Street, this guy came up to me. He said, 'Do you want to come for a ride with me?' I said, 'What do you mean?' He said, 'Come into my car and we'll have a chat.' 'All right then.' I'd clicked. I wasn't stupid. I got into the car and I said, 'Are you gay?' and he said, 'Yes.' I said, 'So am I.' He took me for a drive and got his cock out. I told him to put it away. He said, 'I'd really like to take you out some time.' I said, 'OK but I'm going back in a few days.' He said that there was a pub not far from my hotel. He took me through Soho and drove me to Euston, down King's Cross, to a place called Traffic in York Way. This was going back nine years. It was rough, really rough. He showed me how to get there and drove me back to Oxford Street where I met my mother. She said, 'Where have you been?' I said, 'You know what it's like – a woman shopping!' I'd been away an hour at least. An hour to suss out Soho.

I bought a fab outfit. That night we had dinner. It was about half ten. We said our goodnights and I went to bed. As soon as I went into my room, out came the hairdryer and the brush. I really did myself up. I looked really nice. I actually looked like a boy because I really tried.

I did keep-fit and I'd put some weight on. I had my hair very short. I really made an effort. I had a chubby face. I actually passed as a boy, which was a lot of hard work.

I snuck out, and went into Traffic. It was all I'd dreamed about. Being the centre of attention. When I was walking in, I saw all these men. I looked older than my age, I always have done. At thirteen, I must have looked eighteen. I walked in, went straight to the bar and ordered Malibu and orange. It was the only drink I could think of. I was stood there and everyone went very quiet. I started getting nervous. Oh god, I thought, everyone is looking at me! These old men started coming up to me and chatting me up. I looked over in the corner, and, oh my god, there were these really gorgeous hunky guys playing on the snooker table in the corner. They don't make guys like that nowadays. They were all about twenty-four, twenty-five. While I was having hassles with all these older guys, these hunky guys started looking over and winking at me. I felt good: especially after a couple of Malibus. I was thinking, yes, this girl, she is getting about. One of the hunky guys came over and said he wanted to be chairman of my fan club. I'd really got started on to the scene. I'd made some friends. I never did meet the guy who I'd met that afternoon.

The following Monday I went to the Hippodrome. There I met this guy called Raj who I got really close to. He was half Indian, about thirty-two. He introduced me to the gay scene. He took me everywhere you could think of whenever I came up to London. We played around a bit sexually, but nothing heavy. I kept in touch with him.

I left school at nearly fifteen. It was during the Easter holidays that we emigrated to Spain. My dad bought a bar and restaurant. He was quite wealthy. I helped paint the bar and fix it up ready for the end of the Easter. The plan was for me to go to school there after the holidays. My parents knew I didn't have a good time at school in Wales. I begged them not to send me to school any more. My father was a self-made man, he himself had received little formal education. He always thought that I was going to come into the business and eventually carry it on. He thought he could show me everything I needed to know about the business and so I didn't have to go to school.

38

I did the rent a bit over there. I did it in a different way. There was a big nightclub and a deserted road and I used to stand on the road, and cars would stop. I used to get in the cars, do french or a hand relief, I would charge and get the money.

I was just coming up to sixteen when my dad sold that business and decided to move to run a business in South America. I didn't want to go. We came home to stay with my nan in Leicester for a few weeks, and it was agreed that I could carry on living there with her. I ended up doing this youth training secretarial course. I went to my first course and passed. Then I knocked it on the head, and didn't go back for my second exams. It was doing my head in.

I rang up Raj and said I really want to come to London. He said, 'Fine, I really want you to come and stay with me.' He was living with his wife. I said, 'I can't live with you! What if your wife cottons on?' He said, 'She hardly speaks any English. She won't know anything. She works long hours.' I thought, 'Oh my god.' So I said, 'OK, but remember that this is strictly friendship this time.' I couldn't cope with him sexually. I didn't want to be under his roof and having sex with him all the time.

On the fifth of January '89, aged sixteen, I came to London. Raj picked me up and I went to his house. Everything was fine. I met the wife, she was OK. I had my own room.

Throughout the days he was making passes at me continuously. All the time, it was kiss me, do this. I was thinking this is not me. I started going out to get away from him. I met some friends. One evening, as I was going out, he said, 'You can take your things with you. You are treating this place as a hotel.' I said that I wouldn't be treating this place as a hotel if he weren't always on to me. So he kicked me out; five days in London and I was booted out onto the street.

I'd already met this friend. He picked all my stuff up and I stayed with him a few days and then he took me to Kingston to stay with a person called Howard. He had an employment agency. He put me up at his place. I was sharing with another guy. There was five boys staying there and five girls. They were all working for this agency. I worked there for three months. I was doing at least thirteen hours per day. I had three jobs. I'd get up at six in the morning. I worked for this place serving in the canteen until about midday. It was really nice. I really enjoyed working there. Then from one to six I washed the big pots in another place. Then often from ten till three at night, I'd work in a coat check at a nightclub.

I stuck it for two months. I wasn't even coming out with any money. I had enough to cover my rent. I had to steal food to eat. I hated doing that. I was very desperate at that time.

It wasn't an amusing time. I was working all these hours. There was this man, Howard, who always made passes at me and he even offered me money. It was horrible. He was just renting out his big five-bedroomed house, charging us a fortune on rent, paying us kids a pittance for the agency work, and then charging employers a fortune. He made a fortune out of us. I worked harder than anyone. I had little sleep but I used to sleep all day Sunday, because I never had the money to buy anything to eat. Once I tried renting on the Dilly, but I never saw anything going on. There was nothing happening.

One day I went into Howard's office because he'd conned me over my deposit. I'd already paid my deposit, which he'd taken from my earnings. But he continued to keep taking more money for it. I said I wanted the money owing to me. He said I hadn't paid it. He basically conned me out of a few hundred pounds. I said you can shove this job up your Irish glass, I'm not doing it any more, I'll stay at the place until my deposit runs out, which was about four weeks on. I think I had about £1.50 to my name. I moved out that weekend because I was so unhappy.

That weekend I went off to the Dilly. I got punters all night. I picked one, came back, picked up another and so on and made £60. I had not had that much money for a good three months; £60 was like manna from heaven. I was thinking the next day, I will go out and buy myself something to eat. I can go for a nice meal, I can do this, I can do that, I can go for a drink: £60 of freedom. Every night for the next month I was on the Dilly. I worked till I dropped. When all the boys were chatting away amongst themselves, I was right round the back getting the punters.

40

I was homeless for about a month while working on the Dilly. Every night, I left all my stuff with someone. Every night I got a punter, and I stayed at his place all night. I was very lucky. I'd be out by five in the afternoon. I'd do a couple of early ones, and then look for an all-nighter. I'd charge £50 to £80. If the punter was a really nice guy, I'd say, do you mind if I stay the night? Or they'd ask me if I wanted to stay the night. I'd have dinner and watch telly, have a drink and do the punter. I'd sleep and wake up in the morning and he dropped me back in the West End.

I did very little with punters. I let them play with me, give me a blow job, me play with them, give them a blow job and that was it. In the early days I didn't use condoms with blow jobs, but no one ever came or anything like that. I never ever did penetration. I didn't even entertain it. I heard all these boys saying about how they got fucked by this punter; or I heard this punter saying, I fucked this one and that one. I found I was making the same money if not more than they were. As long as you say this is what you do and this is what you don't do, you'll get business. There's so many boys out there doing everything, because the bastard that's paying them is making them think that's what everybody does. In the beginning I had to say to myself, what do I want to do? I was good-looking and I got money just for being naked with that person. The privilege of letting him see my naked body and mess around and play. I am selling sex, not love: that's serious shit. No tongues, no fingers … it's not love-making. If they want that, they find it for themselves.

I didn't like going with punters. The only ones I liked were the bisexual ones: the rough-looking crowd, the skinheads. They used to love me. The big rough butch skinheads used to be really nice to me; probably because I used to look like a little girl. They were mainly into women, and mostly into having blow jobs. They didn't want to see what I had. I was very frigid. I still am. I clam up. I can't relax. I hated anyone going down on me. When it was with punters I could switch off, but when it wasn't, I was really frigid. Even now. When it's not for money, I can't bear anyone sleeping next to me. Going through the sex part really turns me off.

I met this very rich man in the Golden Lion, who became my sugar daddy. He had five Docklands flats and a big sports car. He was into girls that looked like boys, and boys that looked like girls. He liked me because I looked androgynous. He put me up in one of his penthouse flats. He was basically straight. He treated me like a girl. He was really nice. I only saw him at weekends. We didn't have sex. He'd just take me out for dinners and we'd talk about what it would be like if we had sex.

One of the punters I had was this guy who used to come to see me who had this big cane. I took him back when I was in my flat in the Docklands. I used to beat him. I used to enjoy that. I'd do it to them: never them to me.

On the Dilly, I was wearing a bit of foundation, a bit of mascara, but very natural-looking. I used to wear a big quiff, dress really nice, I was always very effeminate, like a girl. The punters used to walk past me and think I was a girl. I used to go up to them and say, 'Do you want a boy?', and they would say, 'Oh … ?', because I was so pretty. Then, as a boy a lot of them used to like me. When I met the other rent boys on the Dilly they were all right. I never had that much in common with them. I was still pretty much a loner. I was more interested in making my money than chatting away. I wasn't into the drugs or the alcohol or the club scene then – and not now, either. A lot of the boys fancied me on the Dilly. I always attracted the bisexual guys because I was so feminine. I never slept with any of them. I was friendly with them, but not too friendly. I got close to a couple of them, but never too close.

The biggest danger of working on the street is that most of the police view the danger you are in as part of the job: it's a work hazard. Whenever there's any trouble on the street, the police don't give a shit, and you can't go to them. You are always worried about a psycho punter. I've been quite lucky. I've had maybe two or three bad incidents in the years that I have been working. A punter is much more likely to take advantage of someone young and naive than someone who is hardened. When I was new, other boys would take money from me because I was on their patch.

It takes skill to become streetwise, then there's not so much danger. I had to learn to negotiate. It's important to do this before going anywhere with a punter. I'd meet one on the street; I'd be friendly and polite. I'd get straight down to business. I'd ask him what he was looking for and what he wants. He must understand what he's getting for his money. If he says he wants french for £40, I'd say it's going to be £80. Often they'll say that's fine. I overpriced myself and let them knock me down to a price, that I'd sorted out in advance, that would be my lowest.

I've had to learn to be very streetwise. I can tell as soon as I see a guy, whether he's good or not. I pick up vibes. If there was ever a guy on the streets I was not comfortable with, I'd trust my gut instinct and didn't go. If he sounded a bit dodgy, a bit leery or rowdy, forget it. I learnt to get my money before I started anything, as soon as I got in the car. The trouble with driving off to the place and getting the money later, they say, 'Well I've only got £X.' That's how they trap you when you've gone all that way. If they refused to pay me first, I'd make them drop me back. He'd come back round next week, and give me what I asked.

I found doing it in cars wasn't such a good idea. It was risky. You can also get nicked that way. In a car he can do anything he wants to you. The chances are you've not looked at his registration, in the event of trouble, and he can kick you out whenever he wants. I found it best not to go too far from where you are working, and know a place to go to do the business; somewhere quiet and in a back street. The trouble with that is, no one is going to hear anything if there's any trouble. That's where the danger comes in.

I had a bad experience in a car once, we went to a little remote place in the middle of nowhere, he made me do sex and just dumped me there in the middle of the night with no money. I won't get in a car with someone who's got scars and tattoos, or who is drunk. I try to pick a respectable guy. You don't get into a Cortina that's falling to bits. It's difficult to negotiate with a punter who's in a car because all he wants is for you to jump in and drive off. I found it best to have a little walk with them, if possible, and negotiate that way.

I always let them know in advance that I use a rubber for french.

And when you are doing it, to stay in the front seat, stay on top or else they can get a physical advantage over you and you can be trapped.

It's much less dangerous going back and doing it in the punter's apartment, or going back to his hotel. If he hurts you in any way in his apartment, you know where he lives. If he's in a hotel, you know he's on record; you can scream your tits off to security.

All-nighters in hotels are not really that risky, providing you get your money first and hide it. I was working on the Dilly, I was very young, naive and pretty, and this guy came up to me, and he said, 'I want you to come back and stay the whole night in the hotel, I'm staying at Heathrow.' He was well dressed and well to do. I said, 'OK.' He said, 'I'll give you £150.' I thought, 'Oh, fabulous.' We drove there in this nice car, miles out to the hotel at Heathrow. I said to him, 'You must pay me first.' He said, 'Of course I will, I've got a security box at reception, I'll get money out as soon as we get there.'

On the way there, he said he was a pilot, he was really nice. He parked the car in front of reception, he went in, but there was no one at reception. He spoke to a security guard and came back to me and said, 'The receptionist is not on until nine in the morning, the security guard can't give me access to my money, would you mind waiting until the morning? We don't have to do anything tonight.' I said, 'Oh no, you are all right, I trust you.' We had a great time. I made him happy. He was fabulous. All night he kept on telling me, 'Why don't you come to Paris with me tomorrow, you don't need a passport because you'll be with the pilot. Tomorrow you can sit with the crew.' He gave me all that bullshit story. I thought this is a really great punter. We did french twice. He was jolly hard work: but £150 is £150.

In the morning I woke up and he was already dressed. He said, 'Do you want a cup of tea?' I went, 'I'd love one.' He was boiling the kettle and then he went, 'Shit I've already had one cup this morning and there aren't enough teabags. I'll go to reception, get the money and some more teabags.' Did the bastard come back?

I waited for that cup of tea for what seemed like an hour. I thought, 'Where the fuck is he?' I looked around the room, there were no teabags

44

and he'd taken all his stuff and he had left me. He left me in this little hotel in the middle of Heathrow and he hadn't paid me! I thought, 'He's not going to get away with this, he must have given his address to the people at reception.'

So I put everything in my bag: the sheets, the towels, the teapot. I thought, I'll have to get something out of this. Just as I was walking out the room the maid came along; I had to rush back and put everything back. I was asked to leave. I was just miles from anywhere, honey. I was walking in this street and I could see a phone box right at the top of the street. By this time I was actually laughing to myself; whenever I'm in a difficult situation I deal with it by being humorous. I thought, what have I done! I'm miles from anywhere. I just rang everyone. One of my friends was in, and he had a car. Two hours later he finally picked me up and drove me home.

What I normally do with an all-night punter, when he's in the bathroom, I'll hide my money. I find a secure place in the room, where he'll never think of looking, and put my money there, or put it in whatever I'm wearing. I just make sure he's not going to get hold of it, because there is a chance he could be gone, and taken your money back before you wake up.

Now, when I'm going in and out of cars, or just round the corner to a quiet place to do business, I wouldn't even think about leaving my money with 'friends' who are out there with you. No matter how much you trust them, they can run off with your money. It's happened to me! You stash the money in some safe place in your clothing.

The first time I got arrested, I was seventeen and had been on the Dilly for a couple of months. I was really excited. I was walking around Dean Street and Bateman Street. After walking around a few times, I noticed these guys following me. I walked again, and I just knew they were Old Bill. They just got hold of me and said, 'What are you doing?' I said, 'I'm walking around.' They said, 'You are nicked for importuning.' I wasn't importuning; I was looking for a punter. Importuning is when one man actually picks another man up on the streets for sex, regardless of whether money is involved.

45

The first time that you are taken into a police station, you should be cautioned by the superior sergeant or whatever. Then, if you are brought into the station again, you'll be arrested and charged. I didn't know that and they never did that to me. I got taken straight to the police station, charged and put in a cell all night, and in the morning taken to Bow Street Court. I got fined £40 and a criminal record. That was the first of many arrests.

After I'd worked the Dilly for about six months, I started getting really fucked up in the head. I never went out with anyone, apart from for money. I started feeling dirty and used. I kept thinking, why is it that people are doing this to me? It was then I realized I'd never had enough of my innocent time: I lost my childhood too quick.

I didn't have my family around me. The other rent boys were going off and having flings and going to clubs. All I was doing was making money and doing punters; nothing else. I felt cheap. Anyone can have me for £40, £50 or £60. I went through a stage of hating myself for having done it. I got over it. Keeping my self-esteem and self-respect was very difficult. Even now when I think about it, it can get to me now; when I think anyone can pay to go with me.

When I did go with someone that wasn't paying, I didn't enjoy it. I went through the motions, and afterwards I still felt that dirtiness because I hadn't been paid. I felt like I'd done a punter for nothing. Sex was meaningless. There was no love. I was like a hobo.

I was so depressed I started going out. I went to the Apollo club. I was in there when, for the first time, I ever saw a transsexual.

She was a most beautiful, stunning, black transsexual. She came up to me, sat me down, and spoke to me for about two hours. Her name was Trisha. She said to me, 'Honey, you look completely like you've just got to be a sister.' Then, everything I had not understood before suddenly fell into place. I knew then that I was transsexual.

She related to everything that I'd ever felt as woman; I'd never been confident as a boy, I was always nervous, always with my head down. I was unable to make conversation and was very withdrawn. I never felt comfortable being me. I knew being a transsexual was the way I'd always wanted to be. I never knew, until that point, it was possible. It had never entered my head. I remembered when I was little I used to put on my mother's clothes.

I knew I was attracted to men, but never used to enjoy sex, because it never felt right. I would cringe if anyone would go down there. I never went out with anybody and never had a relationship – because it never felt right.

As I continued talking to her, she said to get on the hormones, go ahead as a woman; she could just tell I was going that way. I can look at people now and I can tell they are going to be like me one day.

Always as a boy, I looked like a girl. When I tried to look like a girl, at seventeen, I did everything wrong. Looking like a tart: too much eye-liner, hair back-combed to fuck, six-inch heels I couldn't walk in, tights had ladders in them. You go through that phase: a draggy stage. I started dressing up as a girl at nights and weekends.

I'd started going to Streetwise when I was still sixteen. I heard about it from other rent boys. I went up there nearly every day for a year. It was like a family. It was a place where they would let me live my life and be myself, non-judgemental, but they were always there for help and advice.

I'd been in London about a year, I was seventeen, when my mum came back into the country from South America. I went back to Leicester to see her, to my nan's house. When I saw her, she told me how much she'd missed me. She said to me that she knew something was wrong, that I'd got problems. She could tell. Why didn't I talk to her about it? She genuinely knew something was up. I said, 'I haven't got a problem, just leave it.' Then she just came out with it; she said, 'Is it because you like boys and not girls?' I just started crying, someone had just actually said it. I just started crying and she said, 'It's OK, let's go for a walk.'

We walked to the park. I said to her that I was really sorry. She said, 'What are you sorry for?' She said, 'I love you, no matter what your preferences are, no matter what you are doing, because you are my child.' She said everything just right.

The next thing she asked me was, 'Have you ever wanted a sex change?'

Just like that! I said, 'I've been thinking about it, but I can't seem to make up my mind about it. One minute I do, one minute I don't.' At the time I had many things going on in my mind: I had an unfeminine voice and I was very confused in myself. We had a really good talk. I was really upset because I thought I'd let everyone down, as my father wanted me to carry on the family name and business. She reassured me that none of that was really important. She said she was really sorry for me that I had to carry this burden; I should have spoken to her earlier. She said that she wanted to mention it before, when we were in London once, a long time ago. She said that I'd had something in my pocket, it fell out of the washing. It was a card advertising a gay club. She said she didn't want to confront me with it at that time because, if she'd been wrong, it could have destroyed me. I could have been going through a phase. Even though she knew in her heart of hearts that something wasn't right in my life. She was really fabulous.

We agreed that we wouldn't tell any of the family until I'd had time to have started the treatment and that I was sure that this was what I really wanted. The family were told a year later, when I was eighteen. They were really fabulous. I thought that my father would have taken it the worst. He took it really well. He found comfort in that I wasn't gay. He and I can now really talk. He drives my mother down when she comes to see me. He looks at me as a girl, and calls me Zoe.

Continuing with my conversation in the park: my mother then asked me, 'What are you doing in London?' I said, 'Do you really want the truth?' We'd been so honest; I sort of told her. First of all I told her that I worked for an agency: which was a load of bollocks. Then I said that I met men for dinner, they'd pay me money, and occasionally I slept with them. She looked at me and went, 'Are you being careful?' I went, 'Yes, of course.' She nervously changed the subject. Later, I asked her how she felt about that. She said she didn't like it. She didn't like the fact that out there in London, anything could happen to me. She said maybe she should have held on to me longer.

She said, 'Tell me one thing, if I tell you not to do it, will you stop?' I said, 'No.' She said, 'I'd rather be part of your life no matter what you

48

are doing, rather than you lie to me.' I said, 'No way am I going to give this up; I want things in life, this is the only way I can feel comfortable, the only way I can make money. I'm in a very different kind of scene. I've got to discover myself, to be myself, I've really got to do this.' She was really sympathetic and understanding. She was also very, very worried. I didn't tell her that I worked the streets. I kept that from her for a long time. I just told her that I picked up in bars. If she had known that I worked the streets, she would have put an emotional plea on me. She would have cried, begged me not to do it, and brought me home. I would have gone home because I loved her.

It's only recently I've told her the full story about being a prostitute. She said she felt she was a bad mother. I said that she wasn't. It was just that I was ahead of my years and a very sly little bastard. I was very curious and very good at covering my tracks. Even now, she says to me that I must think she's a bad mother, because she knows what I do.

Before that conversation in Leicester, my mother had no inkling what I was up to. She was really sympathetic. She moved on to speaking to me about changing over and wanting to be a woman. She said to me, the only way that I was ever going to know whether it was for me was to live like that, try it out and dress like a woman. She said she would come down and stay with me. She'd help me out.

She came down and we lived together in my sugar daddy's flat in the Docklands. I still worked. I would just say I was going off somewhere. I worked as a boy and met punters in Victoria or the Dilly. Later, at night, I'd go out as a girl doing the cars in Mayfair and make no money at all!

The other day a girlfriend of mine picked up a client in Harrods and brought him here. We did a double, we said we were girls. She'd had the 'op' and could do the business, I said I 'was on'. When we'd done him and he'd gone, we were talking about the early days when we got into cars along Park Lane. I said to her, 'Do you know what the worst part was; it was my boobs, the padding and trying to give the punter a blow job. His hands were everywhere. I had to make sure he avoided my boobs, and avoided touching my pussy, it was hard work! I got kicked out of quite a few cars when they sussed me!

By the time my mother left me to go back to live with my father, four months later, I was living full-time as a woman. She helped me do my voice, look good and natural, wear stylish clothes. She was really supporting and since I've changed over we've been a lot closer. I was now eighteen.

It was at this time that I discovered a lot of improvements should be made on the NHS for transsexuals. I found the conditions for access for a transsexual to the NHS are made by men. They dictate what a woman should be like, and unless you comply, then you are not going to get your treatment. My reaction to this was that I was not going to turn up for my appointments as they expected: in a pencil skirt, a white blouse and wearing loads of make-up, I'm not going to do other things that stereotype women.

I think that a lot of people who get the NHS shouldn't be getting it at all, they are the ones prepared to collude with the stereotyping of women to get into the NHS system. Whereas a true transsexual will take a stand and say, 'No, I don't think a transsexual should think that's how a woman ought to be. She should be able to wear jeans or other styles of women's clothes.' I think that's why a lot of the true transsexuals, like me, get on their back and pay for it that way.

If you are a young transsexual, and you go on the NHS, you have to go through counselling for two years without being given a hormone. For some people that is good, that's what they should do. For me, once I'd made up my mind, I wasn't prepared to wait to have my operation on the NHS. It would have meant waiting between five and seven years. I know someone who has been waiting twelve.

A lot of transsexuals are thirty or forty years old when they decide to have the operation. They've had a good job, so they've got money to do it privately. For young transsexuals, it's terrible. If you are on the dole you cannot do anything. It's difficult getting the money for the right complete change of clothes, the right help and supervision.

I first got my hormones on the black market. To start off I was taking the right dosage. The first ones I ever took were shit, they were called ethinyloestradiol, an oestrogen. They were really weak and no good.

I never really developed breasts on them until I changed to Premarin. I now also take Provera, a progesterone. It's the best thing I've taken for my boobs.

The hormones, oh god! When I first started taking hormones, I found the depressions horrible. Androcur is taken to suppress the male hormone testosterone in the body. It is used to give male rapists in America a chemical castration. They've stopped giving it to rapists because there were too many suicides, because of the side effects. But it's OK to give it to transsexuals! It can cause severe depression. When I first went on it at seventeen, and I was not producing enough male hormones, I'd just sit and cry all the time. I'd get on the tube and miss my stop. I'd go back and miss it again: my mind was totally deranged the whole time. I got anger bouts where I wanted to lash out at people: it really was a head-fuck, I often felt suicidal. I've stopped taking it now.

A fully grown man is going to need Androcur because a lot of work has to be done to kill the male hormone. It's great for making your hair thick.

I got all the hormones on private prescription when I was eighteen. It's fortunate I started taking my hormones so young because I've not had the problem of facial hair, body hair and my voice was never deep at that age. If I'd waited for the NHS I would have had these problems to deal with.

I had to pay to see a private psychiatrist, which costs £80 an hour. It then costs £60 next time you see him to get a private prescription for your hormones. I've just got a prescription now for two months' supply of hormones, that's going to cost £170.

Some people say that taking hormones takes maybe five or ten years off your life. Having the operation knocks twenty years off your life. But I know transsexuals who are seventy years old. It's not going to put me off. But it can be very dangerous increasing your hormone dosage if you are not careful. You've got to really know what you are doing. I've had hormones prescribed to me now for about four years; never once have they tested my blood for the hormone level. Yet biological women who go for hormone treatment have blood tests to tell them

51

the level of hormone they need. For transsexuals going private and on the NHS, the doctors just prescribe you what they want, and no one gets blood tests.

They cut corners on transsexuals' treatment and make a large amount of money for it. For a sex change operation in London it's £6950 at the moment, soon to be increased. There is one butcher who charges a lot less; although it looks very good, the vagina doesn't work very well, because he chops down your sensitivity bits.

I moved out of my Docklands flat after my mother left. My sugar daddy was pressing me to stop working and stop dressing as a woman. I knew I had to find myself and it was time to go my own way.

I moved in with my oldest friend, Chris. He's always been very compassionate. Always there when I needed help. He's an older gay man. I get on better with older people. That's when I started clipping.

I was out with this tranny friend one night, and she clipped this punter for about £250 and gave me half of it. I thought, oh my god, I've made all this money. I watched the way she did it, and I just developed my style from there. I regret that clipping stage of my life. At that time I wasn't aware that there was any other way you could work as a tranny. I wasn't aware that you could put an ad in the paper. I wanted to be a girl full-time, but I couldn't make any money doing punters in cars dressed as a girl, as I got sussed too easily. I couldn't do anything apart from french because no one could touch my body, I didn't want to work as a boy. I couldn't eat, I couldn't survive. So I clipped. I started ripping punters off. It's bad and I regret it, and I think I've paid my dues for the things that happened.

To clip, I picked up a guy on the street. Best to try to get the tourists. I used to ask them how long they were in town for, and when they were going back. Some people I knew wouldn't give me any trouble. I was really nice to them. I'd say, it's £20 for half an hour, £30 for an hour. I'd explain to the guy that all the girls in Soho work for a madam. She supplies the rooms; some have got a jacuzzi, some have got stereos, videos, hi-fis, some rooms are kinky. They've got bondage racks and all the equipment they could think of. I then took the guy to an office doorway, or any door where there's some stairs.

There, I'd already set up a girl who's in on the scam, she waits downstairs. I'd tell the client that he has to pay the madam before he can go into the room. The guy would say he wanted an hour. The girl goes upstairs to the fictitious madam with the £30. While I was waiting with the client, I'd explain to him that this was not a safe profession. For example, a number of girls got beaten up and a lot of the rooms got damaged. It was expensive and the girl had to pay back the damage caused to the room, the bondage racks, etc. I'd tell him that the madam would probably ask for a security deposit as it was his first time at the establishment. But when he'd finished, and the madam saw that there was no damage, he could sign the register and he'd get his deposit back along with a membership card. So the next time he came by, he could show this card to any girl in Soho and they'd bring him back here.

Then the girl came back downstairs from seeing the fictitious madam. She went, 'OK my darling, the deposit on the girl is £250, and on the room is £250, that'll be £500.' We asked them for a lot more than that as well! He'd say, 'I haven't got that kind of money.' We'd say, 'Of course you haven't! We wouldn't expect you to carry that sort of money.' We asked him, 'Have you any credit cards like Visa, Access; we are not going to take these off you, we just need to check if you do any damage you have the means to pay.' He'd take out his cards, we'd take him to the bureau de change, and told him that we'd got to check to see if he'd got the money. We got him to take £500 out. If at that stage there wasn't enough money in his account, we'd take what was in it.

We'd go back to the doorway, get the money from the client, and say we've just got to show it to the madam to prove that you've got it. Again, I'd wait with him, the other girl went upstairs for a few minutes. She'd come back down and say the madam is busy, but she'd take the money on to the room. I then told him I'd take him on a separate journey to the room.

I would say to him, 'As we are well-known prostitutes, obviously if a policeman sees us entering hotels together, we will get arrested and might not be given bail. You might not get your deposit back.' I'd explain about all the risks. We'd then get to Oxford Street, I'd walk him down a bit and say, 'So, to avoid these risks, I'm going to tell you where to go: if you just wait outside the hotel, the other girl will pull up in a black cab. When she comes out of the cab into the hotel, don't speak to her, just follow her in. You get in the lift, don't talk to her at all, until you are on the floor of the apartment, in case you are being watched.' Then I just sent him off and disappeared!

Some guys just accept they've lost their money, but if one came comes back the next day, I'd say, 'I'm so sorry, darling, we were arrested. If you still want business, you are going to have to do the procedure again with the deposit, because there's a different madam on.' And he'd do it all over again – and sometimes again! These guys can be so naive.

Sometimes I made three or four grand a week. I've worked with some great girls. This is no word of a lie, one girl took a guy for £68,000, that's over the space of six weeks. He was so infatuated with her. You just keep rebooking them and rebooking them, it's one big con that goes on and on.

The police had been keeping an eye on this girl; she was a coke head. They busted her. You'd have thought she would have wasted a lot of that money, but she still had £60,000 left. The police confiscated it, identified the client and wanted the man to take her to court. He disappeared, they found out later he was a member of the IRA. He couldn't turn up in court. They had to give her the money back.

I felt sorry for some of these men: some I didn't. When I ripped these men off for money, I'd convinced myself they were being unfaithful to their wives. It was to teach them a lesson.

We all had a police watch on us for two weeks. We were all rounded up at 7.30 in the morning, twenty-eight of us. It was a laugh. We got arrested, we deserved it. I thought if I'd gone to prison I would have deserved it. They were referring to us in court as criminals, and I'd never seen myself as a criminal.

If I could have worked straight and done punters, I would rather have done that. It's much easier on the mind to deal with. Doing punters isn't nice, but clipping was even worse, because you were robbing people.

I wanted to give the money back to them: a few times I *did* give the money back to them. I felt so sorry for them. I told them it was a big con when I was in the middle of clipping them, when I was away from the other girl, and told them to go.

We got done for conspiracy to deceive. There were separate deception charges and one big conspiracy charge. The conspiracy was very difficult to prove because it wasn't a true conspiracy. It's just as well they didn't prove it: conspiracy is a heavy sentence. They did us for deception. I got given community service: painting and decorating.

I was getting arrested too often, most nights, there were a lot of Tom squad [vice squad] out. I was charged with highway obstruction most of the time. Towards the end they started doing us for importuning. If you get done for importuning you can go to prison.

I was aged eighteen and clipping when I met my first boyfriend. I met him at a friend's flat. I was feeling very lonely and really wanted a man. He was bisexual but more into women. He was Maltese, very sexy and attractive. We flirted all night together. He knew I was transsexual. Then we spent three whole days together, no sex. I fell helplessly in love with him; I was obsessed. On that third day, I'd just got out the shower and he threw me on the bed and ravaged me. I was normally frigid, but this time I wanted it so much. I had anal sex for the first time. It was wonderful. He was the only person I've ever done anal with.

We spent as much time as we could together. He was wonderful to me, made me feel like a woman in every way. He told me he would never hit a woman. A month later I said something that upset him. He got that frenzied look in his eyes, and beat the shit out of me. He didn't stop for what must have been twenty minutes. I had two black eyes, a busted lip and my face was black and blue. I cried out that he had said that he didn't hit women. He said, 'But you are not a woman: you are a man.' That hurt me more than the beating. I knew he'd been beaten up a lot as a kid and had had a very unhappy childhood. Next morning we made it up and I told him I loved him. I thought if I gave him love and kindness, he would change.

Then he lost his job and I supported him. I was very generous, whatever he asked for, I gave him. He was a big gambler: I gave him money every day. He started smoking more and more dope every day: I paid for that. I bought him clothes and cars. He kept me hanging on to a promise – that he would let me know when he loved me. I tried to make that happen. His brothers came to stay and he asked for more and more money for gambling, dope and for them all to go out. They'd get through £2000 in a night. That's where all my money from clipping went. I had virtually no money left for myself. He had become a ponce. I was in a financial trap.

He'd lose at gambling and come home in a foul mood. He'd beat me up again. He kept saying he'd change. I paid for him to go to counselling. He didn't turn up for the appointments. I was in an emotional trap. I loved him and felt sorry for the unhappy childhood he'd had.

On my nineteenth birthday, I had to go to court. That morning, he flew into one. He kicked the bathroom door open, grabbed me and kept banging my head against the bathroom door. I flew into a rage and started hitting him. He kicked and punched me down the stairs and I flew out the house in my dressing gown and no slippers. He came after me and continued battering me. No one stopped to help. I got to a phone box and rang the police. They came straight round and took us both to the police station in separate cars. He was arrested for ABH. The police looked after me so well. The doctor gave me painkillers. Then came the sting; he had charged me with assault. The police were very sympathetic to me, but they said there was nothing they could do about his charge. In the end I dropped my charges. He could be so nice; I'd think about his childhood and I forgave him.

After the conspiracy affair I worked as Lolita, a schoolgirl, for four months. I had my hair in pigtails, wore a school uniform and the punters thought I was fifteen. It was before I had boobs because the hormones hadn't worked. I had these two large nipples and two tiny lumps. As I was doing my act I'd say, 'Wait until you see my little boobies', and when they saw them they'd gasp and go, 'God, you really are like a schoolgirl, you've barely got any.' I stripped off to my really tight knickers. I used to have this really good tuck, pulling the penis back tightly between

56

the legs, and they'd be down there, licking right into my thighs. I used to be laughing to myself so much, 'God, they don't know I'm a boy!' They didn't suss me once. It was such a kick for me at that time and it was so good for my confidence as well. I used to tell them, 'I'm not taking my knickers off'. That was part of the kink – part of the school uniform had to stay on. They wanted a fifteen-year-old schoolgirl and that's what they saw.

Honest to god, these punters would believe anything. All they wanted was something different, anything different. I swear if I had three boobs they would have been queuing up. I saw about ten clients a day, five days a week. The most I did in one day was seventeen. The first couple of punters in the day and I'd be nervous. I just did hand jobs and french, charging £30 to £80 a time.

I did Lolita with this big fat tranny in west London. She was enormous, and if there was ever any trouble she'd just come in and wallop them, tell them to get dressed and leave. We advertised by ad in the paper. She answered the phone. She got half the money, which was a real bummer; she really did me, I did all the work.

I worked from ten till midnight. We didn't normally do anything until three o'clock, and from then on it was chaotic. I'd have times when four of them were waiting on the couch in the living room and I'd be doing one in the bedroom. I went back and forth, back and forth, trying to rush each one, to get to the next one. It wasn't difficult; not many men last for more than two minutes anyway! No sooner had I got down to two in the living room, the doorbell would ring and another one would come in.

They'd all just sit there, no one looked at anyone, no one talked to anyone. It was like sitting in a doctor's surgery. One would look at the fireplace, one would look at the picture, one would pretend to read a magazine, they'd drink a cup of tea. They were all there for the same reason and no one really cared about seeing each other there. Imagine how embarrassing it would be if it was their brother or their boss! Or if it was the boyfriend of one of my girlfriends. I'd tell her to start charging him for it!

57

The work was good for the adrenalin, seeing all that money coming in. It was fierce, very tiring.

During my time as Lolita, I got my flat together with my boyfriend. When it was ready I started working from home as a tranny by putting ads in the paper and through the agencies.

I sometimes made £3000 a week. The money rolled in. It all went on cars, gambling and the flat. He found out I'd saved £3000 for my breast operation. He battered me for that; he wanted another car. I had the operation when I was twenty. He had calmed down and I was over the moon. It was a wonderful success and I became a 36C.

The first time I got robbed was by junkies in our flat in south London. They must have got my number from a card in a window, phoned me up and pretended to be a punter and got my address. Then they turned up on another day, in the middle of an afternoon, when I wasn't working, on my day off.

The doorbell went. I opened the door. I was still in my dressing gown. There was a man standing there. He said to me, 'I called earlier.' I said, 'You couldn't have called earlier because I'm not working today.' And then I looked at him and he looked at me, and then he clicked and I clicked. I tried to slam the door in his face and he booted it open. About four of them came in with him, they had knives and bottles. They held me at knife-point. My boyfriend was there at the time. He ran down the stairs to try and help me, and they battered him. They put towels over our heads. We couldn't look at them, it was really terrible. They got away with about a grand in cash and my jewellery. They ransacked the flat.

Towards the end of it, one of them came in, and he'd remembered what was on my ad. He went, 'You're a fucking man, aren't you!' I just had this dressing gown on. I'd just got out the bath. I had nothing on underneath. Two of them tried to get my dressing gown off, and, just at that time, one of my friends rang the doorbell. The bastards must have thought it was the 'Old Bill'. I thought to myself, what if they'd ripped that dressing gown off me, they would have cut my tackle off: given me the quickest sex change ever! I can laugh about it now, but I was petrified.

58

I also think, thank god I had money and jewellery in the flat, something to take, otherwise they might have got so frenzied, they would have stopped at nothing. They could so easily have slashed my throat or my face.

After that we got a dog. Now, I always keep some money in the flat, even if it's just £100, and a baseball bat. I never answer the door to anyone unless it's by appointment.

I found out later, these guys had done fourteen girls' flats in south London. They raped two of the girls and slit one girl's throat. I was lucky: saved by the bell. I heard the police were after them. I don't know if they ever got caught.

I didn't actually go to the police about that. I had just given up the Soho shit and I hated the police. I thought they wouldn't help me. I actually got a call from them asking me if this incident had happened to me. If it had, they wanted to help me. I wish now that I had said yes. It was the thought of inviting the police into my place. The police are funny that way; they'll come in to help you get the gang that you want, then six months later they'll say, 'let's pay her a visit'.

My boyfriend met this girl in the park while he was walking our dog. He had affairs with many girls, but this time he told me to move out the flat; his name was on the rent book. He told me I could never be a woman and never have kids. That hurt the most. I moved straight out of that relationship and never missed him one bit. I suffered a lot of violence, much of it too painful to think about. I don't regret that relationship. I learned that never again was anyone going to treat me like that. I learned what self-respect meant. I knew I was better off on my own, and that I could take care of myself.

Looking back, working the street was no fun: out there in the cold and the rain. But there was nothing like the adrenalin rush caused by the danger. The best rush of all was when I was working on the streets in Santa Monica, Los Angeles, when I was just turned twenty-one years old, just after the break-up of my relationship. There was a few-mile strip with nothing but trannies working. It was such a kick because there were all these trannies and girls on this Hollywood boulevard. They were wearing thigh-length boots, just coming out in bras and knickers. They were outrageously dressed; everyone was a real exhibitionist and so we joined in. It was so far away from normal life. We were walking up and down, and cars were pulling over all the time, going in and out of them all the time. You could still get busted and nicked. It was all hustling and a lot of danger. It was so cheap and nasty. We loved it.

I got robbed at gunpoint there. I went with this tranny friend. We both worked this street, just for the fun of it. She met this guy who was heavily into crack. I told her not to take him back to our room. But one thing led to another and she did.

Before I knew it, this same guy returned with a stranger and came straight in our room, and smacked me over the head with a gun. They tied me up and pointed the gun in my mouth. It was awful and what was so really scary about being held up by the gun was the fact that they were on crack. You see people in films, and they are really off their head, they are in such a frenzy. Any little thing could upset them. They could have pulled that trigger at anything.

My friend was arguing with them and I thought, oh my god, just shut up. We are going to get shot. It was so frightening. I just put my head down praying. It was then I saw my life flash past before my eyes, knowing it was my time to go.

They robbed us of everything. I'd taken about £1500 out there with me for the two weeks. It was all changed into dollars. I'd spent about £1200 on myself and presents, and it was all taken.

After that, all I wanted to do was go home. I was so angry with my friend, because she'd literally brought this on to us through her own stupidity. I had no money, I had to buy all those things all over again. My friend lied. She said we could make a thousand dollars a night on the street. Bollocks, it was more like a hundred dollars a night: five or six cars at twenty dollars a time. This time it wasn't a case of going out on the street because I wanted a bit of fun and extra money. I had to work the beat because I had absolutely no money; it was horrible.

On my return, I earned enough to put a deposit on a luxury two-bedroomed flat in Earls Court. I wanted to work in style from the flat, and have my mother come to stay regularly. I started really getting it together by this time. I advertised as a transsexual masseuse and escort and also worked through a transsexual agency. Agency clients are really good. Transsexuals have become big business now because it's so unusual. We are making more money than the guys, and a lot of us are making more money than the women out there. Lately though there's been a whole load more on the scene, some of them doing everything for £30.

This year, the recession has hit me. The clients are still there, but they want it for less. A couple of years ago, you used to get at least once a month a client who'd give you a grand or so. Now they haven't got it.

I knew I wanted to go a long way with my work, because I could make a lot of money in the business. I planned on going legal in the new tax year: quite simple because being a masseuse is legal. I'm very ambitious. When I'm thirty I want to be very rich. I want to be successful. I want to own my own place. I don't want to sell sex just to survive. I need to have some purpose to lie on my back. I've started doing tax-free savings plans which I've invested over twenty-five years. I'm going to do pension schemes and short-term savings plans and some bonds. When I'm legal, I will be in a position to do really big financial things like investing fifty grand in a bond or stock.

I have a client who's in the financial business. He gives me my financial advice. He's a well-known person in the financial world. You'd read about him in the *Financial Times*. He's about thirty-two, with the most sexy, cheeky face you've ever seen. Really typically good-looking and he's so charming. He's one of my favourites. He comes in, we sit and drink, kiss and cuddle. I actually enjoy kissing him because he's so cute. We lie in bed for about two hours. All we do is kiss and cuddle and he licks my boobs. He keeps his underwear on: I keep mine on. He doesn't even have an orgasm. After he's gone I feel like I've had twenty orgasms. I'm the first prostitute he's been to.

He came here by mistake. He came here thinking I was a girl: he just didn't look the transsexual type. I said to him, 'What got you into transsexuals?' and he said, 'What does that actually mean?' He thought it was girls who service girls and guys. I've got a few clients who allow me to keep my knickers on, they know it bothers me. They are the sort of men I respect and I don't mind doing. They are the only clients I can have as good regulars. If the client is really into the sex thing I can't be doing with it.

Most of my clients are married. I think a lot of people in marriages are not very happy. I think that a lot of guys who come to a transsexual like the idea of a cock, but not of a guy. So going with me they've got that, and so they don't feel too guilty. For clients it means they are not completely queer. They say to me, 'You are a woman with a cock.' I say, 'Please, darling, tell me one woman you know born with a cock!' These men actively seek a transsexual. The funny thing is that it doesn't matter how gorgeous you are; how big your boobs are; they just don't want to look at them. Most of them aren't even half interested in that. So I don't really like working as a transsexual; I prefer to work as a woman. It does get me down. Some of them are quite obnoxious in what they want. I think to myself, why don't you go to a man? They say, 'Why can't you fuck me? Can you do this and that?' And I say, 'No, I can't.' I often think to myself, if they admit to being homosexual they would be a lot happier.

They ask for everything: from domination, humiliation, straight, some come in for french, toe-sucking. Guys have got off smelling my shoes: my shoes do stink a little I must say! I don't like people wanting me to fuck them, or come on them, or disgusting things like that. I won't use down there.

A few months ago, my doorbell went. I looked out the window, there were all these very official-looking men there, not in uniform, just plain clothes, very official-looking. I panicked and thought, Oh god, it's the council tax people! I panicked. I didn't answer it. They went away. I went downstairs, but nothing was put through the letterbox.

About an hour later, my landlord phoned me and said, 'I've got to speak to you. There's a big problem. People from Scotland Yard have been in to see me.' I thought, oh my god. He came round and said it was something to do with a rape in south London. They were wanting to see my file and anything he had on me. Not only that; they dropped me right in it. They said to my landlord, we want to speak to the *man* living in his property at … The landlord doesn't know I'm transsexual. He said, 'There's no man living there. I have a woman in that flat.'

When he came round he still hadn't clicked. I think he's a bit slow. The police told him I was a prostitute; but he already knew.

Then he told me they wanted me to help them with information. I ask you, is that the way they should go about getting me to help them? They could have got me evicted. I felt sick to the stomach. I didn't know what was happening. What have I done? Any person from the law makes me go a bit funny anyway. Then I called Scotland Yard, and they didn't know anything. I called the Home Office, and they didn't know anything. About eight o'clock that evening, I got a phone call from a police station in south London. They said Scotland Yard were involved but it was being investigated at their station. They told me a guy called _____ had raped quite a few women; some really badly, doing really horrible things. The suspected rapist had told them I was his girlfriend!

He had told them I was a prostitute, and that's how he'd met me. He said that he was in love with me, and that I was his girlfriend. They told me he was into wearing women's underwear, how he wore it, and they wanted to get a character profile.

They came round the next day, showed me a picture of him. He had been to see me quite a lot. I remembered him but I don't remember what we did or said. I can remember his face and I can remember seeing him. But for some unknown reason, I can't remember a damn thing. That was weird; I always remember clients. Someone can ring me up and say it's so and so with the pink tie, and I'd remember everything, what we did and how much he'd paid. It was probably when they told me, I got so nervous, I had a mental block.

I'd seen him loads of times. To this point now, my mind is a blank. All I can remember was that he was really sweet. The police asked me a load of questions. They said the dates he raped were the dates he'd given them when he'd also come to see me. He kept a diary. Apparently he came to see me either just before or just after he'd done a rape.

He told them everything about me. They knew every address I'd had.

Every phone number, every ad I'd placed; everything you can imagine. Scotland Yard had got a big thick file on me. Believe me, if you think Scotland Yard hasn't got a file on you, honey, believe you me, they have.

Apparently he was confessing to all these horrible things, and he went into great detail. The police now knew I was a prostitute. They thought I was his girlfriend; seeing him all the time and dating him. For one horrible minute, I thought they were going to turn around and say I knew all about it. Can you imagine, all I needed was to sit there, and for them to say, 'The rapist said that you'd staked them out for him.' I'd have died. That was all pretty scary.

Five months ago, I moved out of Earls Court. I'd decided the time was right for me to have my pussy done. I booked it four months ahead and I had to earn the £6950 to pay for it plus another £3000 to get another flat and to keep myself for another two months after the op, as I'd be unable to work. The upkeep of my flat was too high for me to save that kind of money, business had not been good. I moved back in with my old friend Chris and worked from there. I paid him so much per client for my rent. I worked non-stop. I worked to the point of exhaustion. In two months I'd saved £4000.

Then, this fabulous man came back into my life. He'd always adored me and always wanted me. He was rich, kind and caring. He helped me out with the rest of the money I needed. He gave me money to move into my new flat. He gave me lots of love and support.

I got my pussy six weeks ago, created by a most fabulous London surgeon. It was a piece of cake! My HIV test, which they do at the same time, came back negative. The surgery is an amazing success, it looks wonderful. I've had fifteen orgasms so far. At the age of twenty-two, I feel so happy at last.

RIP: Zoe met a tragic end after being with a punter in her flat.

'Paul'

I am twenty-one years old. I spent my first seven years in Bridgend, in my nan's house, with my mum, my nan and my cousin Rob. It was the same house my mum was born in. My nan had eleven kids, nearly all girls. My mum was the second to last born. She worked as a nurse and did shifts. Rob, who was much older than me, lived with us while my Auntie Meg worked as a prostitute in Birmingham.

I had a really close relationship with my nan. She was everything to me. I didn't really care about anyone else, as long as my nan was there. She was always there for me. I feel guilty saying this. My mum was rushed off her feet, working. I think she was jealous of our relationship.

Birthdays: I remember the front room, the coal fire. My nan used to have this big, really old, china plate. She used to fill it with fairy cakes and sponges with Smarties and chocolate buttons. I used to have fab parties. Loads of games. All my cousins next door would come to my nan's. We knew everyone, all the kids in the street, they would come down. It was really nice.

There were always loads of presents because it was a big family. I remember my Auntie Liz and Uncle Don bringing me this rag doll, and my mum she went mad. She became my favourite doll, Madge, I called her – after my nan. I used to have dolls, prams, cots, the lot. I got dolls because that was what I asked for. I had hundreds of dolls. I used to play with them, feed them, I used to love my dolls.

I was bought Action Man. My cousin, Julie, next door used to have Barbie dolls and I used to steal the dolls' clothes to put on my Action

Man. My friend Hilary had a brother who was in the army. Her mum told my mum that he used to play with dolls as well. She told my mum not to worry, it was just a phase I was going through.

I woke up one morning, went to my cupboard in the kitchen with all my toys in, and all my dolls were gone. I was hysterical. My mother had burned them. I don't know why: I think she was going through a hard time; she had a complex about me and my dolls.

My first week in junior school, aged five, I remember taking sandwiches to school. My nanna said that you have to wait until the big school before you can take sandwiches. I remember asking Julie if I could take sandwiches for school and she said yes. I was up really early and made them in secret. I made sandwiches with lard. I thought lard was butter. I put Milky Ways in my lunch box. I was all excited going to school. When I got to school my sandwiches were foul.

I really enjoyed school in Bridgend. I really got into it and I got on.

Then, when I was seven, me and my mum moved to Neath. I hated it. I wasn't even told that I was moving from Bridgend. My Auntie Sheila and three older cousins lived in Neath. I was told that we were going to stay for a few days with them and that was it. I hardly knew them. I hardly saw my mum. She was working at a service station. She was working most nights and sleeping most of the day. My Auntie Sheila was hardly there either, and so it was mostly my three older cousins who looked after me.

I didn't like any of the subjects at school. I was in the proper classes at first, and then, a year later, I was in the remedials. It was awful. I got picked on by the other kids.

I pined to be back at my nan's. My mum didn't have time to be with me. She'd met this guy, Bill, and so it was her and him, her and him: no time for me. Otherwise she was doing the washing, or making tea for other kids coming over.

She used to get the others to take me out. I pined for my nan. If I'd been left there, my life would have been very different. I was very lost a year later, I always thought we were going back.

I was always on a high at my nan's. When I was out playing on my bike, and I grazed my knee, my nan was always there. I knew loads of people and most of my family were there. In Neath, I sank into a huge, long depression. I had nothing to do. I started getting into trouble.

When I was eight, we moved into a caravan. That was awful. There were rats outside. Bill used to come and stay. He didn't have what I wanted from a dad. He was a kid and my mum mothered him. He was my rival, but he got all the attention. I couldn't get to my mother. I'd get back from school and he'd be back. I never had any time on my own with her.

Then, a year later, we moved to the other side of town. Bill and my mum rented it. It was a huge place, a big old house, and just fields and fields. There were no other kids around. I didn't have any friends out there. I used to go for long walks. I found loads of things to do: chasing pheasants, thieving kittens from farms and telling my mum I'd found them. I used to get chickens and lock them up; they used to die. I used to stick chickens into the bonnets of tractors, I shoved a dog in the cattle dip. I used to get my dog, Tess, to chase the sheep. Then I got found out. I had to have my dog put down for savaging them. She was my companion for a year. I was a bastard, the things I used to do. I knew it was wrong.

I was a bastard towards Bill. He used to repair things in his garage. I used to break his machinery. I used to cut the tubes on his compressor. I played around with his soldering iron. I used to break things on purpose. He used to batter me when he found out. He chased me up the stairs, put me over his knee and gave me a few slaps. In the end I got used to it. I was getting more bollockings than god knows what. That's when I first started to stutter. It happened when he was shouting at me. I got hysterical. He'd explain why I was getting the bollocking, then I'd get it, but I was never allowed to explain myself. I did it because I was bored. Like I say, I was in the middle of nowhere, nobody around except my dog, my mum was out cleaning all day in some hotel, and Bill was out working. So I was left with no one.

I doubt if Bill saw me as a rival. He did try with me after a while. He used to take me to work with him on the JCB, but I wasn't really into it. He used to take me horse-riding. But by that time it was too late and I didn't want to know him.

After Tess was put down, my mum got me a bike. When I had my bike it was much easier to get around. I started riding off and seeing different friends.

I was ten when my Auntie Margaret and Uncle Alex came to stay for a few months. It was really fab. I had a really good relationship with Uncle Alex. He used to take me to school and collect me, instead of me making the hour journey home by school minibus. He used to buy me presents like pencils and things like that. He was really sweet. I think he was the first person I fell for. He was just like how a dad should have been. I felt a lot closer to him than knowing Bill for three years.

I was ten when my mum and Bill got married. I had a good feeling about having a new brother. That didn't last long. I started getting pissed off and jealous. Family and relatives saw me as the odd one out. No one had time for me. I wasn't really wanted and I wasn't part of their family. I started breaking things, causing trouble, hoping that I would get sent to my nan's. But my mum wouldn't have it. She wanted everyone to think that we were one happy family.

I went to comprehensive when I was eleven. I made a load of friends, mostly girls. I started shoplifting, smoking and skiving from school. I'd sneak out at night and we'd go thieving. We could go out of school at dinner times and most of the time I didn't bother coming back. I used to go drinking, stealing people's dinner tickets and use them to buy rolls and sweets. We used to spend our dinner money on cider and cigarettes. My mum used to get called into the school quite often. She'd have a go at me in front of the teachers, but then she'd be fine when we got back home and have a laugh with me about it.

I remember when I was just twelve, I was watching television and there was a prostitute in it. It was about a brothel. I thought to myself that was what I wanted to do. I got butterflies and thought, my god, I want to do that. Not for the money, I would have done it for nothing. It just really appealed to me. Having sex with all the men really appealed to me. I didn't even know what sex really was.

I knew my Auntie Meg was a prostitute from when I was really young. My cousins used to call her 'fucking prostitute'. I used to like her. She'd been selling herself for years and I think it's affected her; like I think I've been affected. I used to find her really funny. Whenever she used to come down from Birmingham, we used to always have a good time. She used to bring all this money down. She used to treat me. We had a good relationship.

When I was young, my cousins used to call me a bastard, saying I hadn't got a dad. It wasn't really a big thing, but by the time I was twelve I started thinking a lot about it. I knew I wanted a dad. I knew I liked men. I was very mixed up. I really didn't know what was going on. I remember hearing my mum talk about Auntie Meg when she turned lesbian after having her kid. She said it made her feel sick, she was really anti-gay. Then she used to tell me when I got older that men are only good for money and sex. I really thought a lot about that comment. I did like the idea of sex with men. That's when I started thinking about wanting to have a man to buy me things; this is what it meant to have a dad. I was very confused inside. I felt such a freak. I phoned up Childline but in the end I actually told them I wanted to go back and live with my nan; they couldn't help me.

I was arguing constantly with my mum. I felt like some kind of pervert. I thought I was sick in the head. I thought I was the one and only male who felt like this about other men. I wanted to stop liking them. My mum didn't know how to handle me. I tried to hang myself a couple of times. I threw a rope over a branch and tried to do it. The other time, I tried to strangle myself with some string from my hood. I felt no one understood me, and I didn't understand myself.

I was thirteen when I met Anna. I fell in love with her. I was obsessed. We met on a bus. Me and my friend John were getting on a bus near a naughty boys' home. Anna and her friend thought we were from there. They thought we were real men – geezers. Then we started talking, and I walked her home. It was miles up this hill. We got really close. It was the first proper relationship that I had had. At first, I wanted a girlfriend because that was the proper thing to do. But not so long after that,

I really got into her. I enjoyed it. I told her I was bisexual. She didn't know what that meant.

We started getting into loads of shit. Shoplifting and things like that. Me, John, Anna and her friend, we went into this church to see what we could steal. I found a sack. I remember taking it and shaking it. I ran outside and emptied the bag and there was all these envelopes full of money. When we shared it out, I blackmailed everyone saying, if you give me half what you've got, I'll take your blame if we get caught. I had more than anyone, I was rolling in it.

I managed to spend a lot of it on silly things: sweets, pens, pencils, rubbers, cigarettes, taxi fares. I also chucked away hundreds of pounds for fear of getting caught. I chucked it down drains and left it in telephone books. But John got flash with his money. He got found out. Next thing I knew, the police were round at my house. My mum was crying. I went to school next day and I was expelled. I had to go to court, it was awful. Out of the four of us, I ended up with the smallest fine; even though I'd taken the most money. It was because I cried in court. I cried because my mum was poking me in the back. My mum paid my £80 fine. I wasn't allowed to see Anna after that.

A short while after this, the guy who sorts it out when you skive off school, and my social worker, met with my mum. God knows what they'd been talking about. They told me they said they were going to send me to a children's home for a few weeks to give my mum a break. They packed me off to this awful place.

I had to share a dorm with fifteen other guys. At thirteen, I was easily the youngest. I should have gone into a children's home, but because there were no spare places I went into the next thing before prison. I was bullied there. I got a black eye the second day I got there. I was sat around this table first thing in the morning with all these yobbos who were about eighteen or nineteen. One of them spoke to me and I ignored him. The next thing I knew, I went flying off my stool. I'd just been punched. I remember my legs hitting the top of the table.

There, we went to school and church. In the morning we had to clear out the chickens, collect the eggs, set the table, polish your boots, then you had to go to an assembly. We did woodwork. We had to paint a fence; it was the first time I'd ever sniffed and enjoyed paint. People used to just piss about.

My first night there, I could do nothing but cry. Everyone was asleep and I was just lying there, covered in snot, in a right state. The thing that really upset me was that I wasn't even allowed to wear my own underwear. I didn't have anything to remind me of home.

It was awful, especially in the night-time, loads of sex going on. There was this ginger guy there, I hated him, he was always playing with himself. I wasn't too naive to know what was going on.

Loads of boys were being sexually abused there. My bed was facing this ginger guy, he was about twenty-one. He had this other guy over in his bed. They were messing about under the sheets and I thought they knew I was a poof and were trying to suss me out. There was loads of sex going on: there was sex in the showers. You'd walk into this room, there was a wall and the shower was behind this wall and two guys who were running the place used to stand there watching the boys showering. It was awful.

I was sat in the dorm at dinner time. I'd made some stupid bit of wood and stuck my name on it. I was going to give it to my mum when she came to visit me. This ginger guy came over to me over, started using words like 'gobble' which I'd never heard of. He started to come on to me for sex. I was terrified. I was being bullied in lots of other ways there.

There was a woman who used to work there and she used to do the dinners. She was really sweet. I told her what most of the boys were doing. She told me to keep myself to myself. She knew what the boys were doing to the boys in there, that's why she took me under her wing. In the evening, after tea, we'd go fishing or for a walk. She used to take me to her house, give me chocolate; if it wasn't for her I would have really cracked up.

I told my mum and Bill, when they come to visit, how awful it was. They said right, you are coming home. They had an argument with the guy in the office. I heard him say, 'No, he's not leaving.' My mum said, 'Well I signed him in and so I can sign him out.' I got taken out

71

of there; I'm telling you, that sorted me out for some time. I was as good as gold for weeks.

I used to stay at my nan's in Bridgend quite often. Every time I went down there I was on a high. Every time I came back to Neath, it was one big depression. I had nothing to do apart from getting into trouble. This particular time, I was sent down to stay at my nan's, still aged thirteen, because I was going through another real bad patch with my mum and Bill. I believed that they didn't want me and I was in the way, as usual.

I was waiting for a bus in the bus station. There was a toilet. This guy was looking and beckoning to me. I seen him coming in and out of the toilets, and then I followed him in and started talking to him. He asked me if I wanted to come for a drink. I said, yes, where? He said, in the pub. I thought, I'm not old enough. We had a drink. He then took me to a quiet spot by the river, by a tree. He then started frenching me and I went straight down on him. I was well away. I knew what to do, I didn't believe it. He gave me eight quid and his phone number. When I got to my nan's, I was so sick. I washed out my mouth with soap. I felt so guilty.

When I met this man, I was looking at him as a father, which I wanted more than anything. I thought that sex was love and that he was showing me love. I wanted it and enjoyed it in a way. In another way it turned me. I felt really guilty towards my mum and my nan. I felt like I'd betrayed them. I seen him a few times after that.

My mum drove me up to London to stay with my Auntie Meg, who was now a prostitute in London. I stayed for three days. I wandered off on one of these days and went to Piccadilly Circus. I wanted to see the prostitutes. I got stopped by a policeman. He asked me what I was doing; I looked a bit young to be around there. I said to him that I was staying with my auntie in Barnes. He told me to be on my way or I'll end up in trouble. I went back to my auntie's. I'd seen what I wanted to see, and I knew I'd be back. I was all excited and got butterflies at the thought of it. I went back to my nan's by train.

I got back to Wales and I seen my mum's car outside my nan's. I walked in and my mum was crying. I knew I'd got found out. I'd told my auntie in London about the guy on the river bank and she'd told my mum. The police were called in, and I had to go down to the police station to describe this guy's bedroom. I remember Bill had been through my clothes and found his phone number and rang him up and screamed down the phone at him. That really pissed me off. I thought that the guy was being a father to me and was giving me love. I was really pissed off with my mum, it seemed like anything I cared about, she took them away from me: my nan, my dolls, my dog, Anna and now this guy. There was no one I could trust.

Very recently I seen this guy's face on *Crimewatch*, I got the shock of my life! He was wanted in connection with a series of rapes.

I had another huge argument with my mum after Christmas when I was just fourteen. I was hitching a ride from Neath to my nan's. As I walked down this carriageway, a guy picked me up. He told me he was a psychic. He drove me into this lorry park and we frenched each other. It cheered me up. I thought this was a new way to have fun. I got him to drop me off a bit further up the carriageway, and then I hitched back and picked up another guy. He took me into this big field and he had a groundsheet which he put down. That was horrible. He rimmed me [licked around the anus]. Then he drove me back to my mum's.

I started hitching at night quite often, most nights. I would always pick up at least one person in a night. I'd hang around the services and pick up lorry drivers and they'd do it in their cabs and they'd pay me money. My mum worked nights and I used to sneak in so Bill wouldn't hear me.

While I was still fourteen, I told my mum I was running away. She gave me the money for the fare. I got the train and arrived in Paddington. I sat down on a red stool where all the taxis drive out of the station. I sat next to this guy who was reading a paper with money pinned inside it. He asked me what I was doing. I said I was on my way to my auntie's, but didn't know how to get there. He said he'd got an *A–Z* in his house. He drove me there. He got me on to his bed. I froze. I was really scared. I kept thinking people would come in. In the end he just frenched me. He paid me and showed me where the road was on the

A–Z and took me back to Paddington station. He said next day he'd show me where all the gay clubs were. I was really excited. Next day he wasn't there. I later found out that this guy was the boyfriend of a very famous woman singer and hung around here regularly.

Back at Paddington I went to the cottage. That's when cottages were cottages. I couldn't believe it. There were fifteen men around the pee bar. All sorts was going on. I stayed there for three days, made loads of money. Punters didn't want much: just gropes, blow jobs, and looking at my bum. Nothing really serious. I think I wanted to do more than they did. I think they were really wary about how far they could go with me, because I was so young.

Then I met this skinhead. I went back to his. He had a boyfriend. I had sex with him and his boyfriend. He asked me if I'd done punters. He was living in this house in Seven Sisters, with three other rent boys and this guy who was a punter. He took me back there. There I met Den, my first boyfriend. He had a 'tache and he was doing punters as well.

He was the first guy I ever did anal with. It was awful but nice. That was love, love, love. I was so in love with him. He was a right pisshead; cans of Special Brew. He introduced me to poppers. I thought he was trying to kill me.

I made a fortune there. I spent it all on sweets. I was still only fourteen. I was introduced to a regular punter called 'Shit Anton'. He would lie there with a toilet seat over his face and the lid up, and I would have to shit into his mouth, £50 a time.

Den and I had a big argument about money. I left there and another guy took me to meet punters on a certain platform on the Euston underground station. I slept in an underground car park or was kept at various punters' houses. I was very much in demand because I was so young.

I met Len, a punter, when I first come to London – in the Golden Lion. He was nasty. I did him a few times. He took me back to his place. He was about sixty. He did something really posh, to do with grammar schools. He was really kinky. He liked to have his nipples really pulled, and would say bite my nipple, and it was already bleeding. I used to ride him really, really hard and he used to say, 'Go on, Red Rum, go on, Red Rum, go go go.' He was lying face down into the bed, I'd be playing with his nipples, him with his arse in the air. A horrible sight. He was a dirty bastard; he used to want to get into piss, but I could never do that with him. He was a cheap bitch, he paid £35. Actually, I'm not sure what Red Rum is.

Then there was the one with the cream cakes. He was one weirdo I'm telling you. I was with some boy around Earls Court. Some guy pulled up in a plush car, he obviously was the chauffeur. He took us back to this huge, posh place. We were taken into this room with all of these coloured leather pouffes. This old guy came in with all of these fresh cream cakes on this big tray. He was like Santa Claus, really jolly. We had to jump like bunny rabbits over the pouffes while he sat there trying to throw cream cakes at our bare bums. It wasn't sexual. He was hysterical, absolutely loving it. I got paid quite a bit for that – about £60. It was the most I'd ever had at that time.

I didn't call my mum for four months. I rang her and she was hysterical. She was really upset. She thought I was dead. During this time I'd wanted to speak to her desperately, but I thought she hated me and didn't want me. I was a mistake in her life. I thought she had what she wanted, Bill and my baby brother. So, I made sure that I enjoyed London. She asked me to come home. I went back to Neath, winter was starting.

I started knocking around with Anna again. She came to stay at my home because her mum and dad were divorcing, and her dad was a real bastard. He had been doing things to her. She just did not want to be there. Her mum agreed she could come and stay at my mum's. She stayed with us for a few months.

Then, when I was fifteen, Anna and I went off to London together. We got to London, we were walking about, and then we met Lee. He was outside Heaven, wearing tight black jeans, wild black hair all over the place, loads of make-up, looking so camp. I just had to talk to him. We chatted to him and this girl, Juliette, for a bit and they took us back to their squat in Tufnell Park.

Next morning Lee took us shopping. He stuck a rucksack on my back and one on his. He took us into the shop and told the girls to walk behind us and fill up the rucksacks.

That night Lee got us into doing Pro-Plus [over-the-counter caffeine tablets] and smoking plasticine. I thought my god, I'm such a junkie. I really believed I got a high off it. I didn't start real drugs for a while after that.

I didn't like shoplifting. It was getting me paranoid. I didn't want any more trouble with the police. I'd been done for shoplifting before, there was the trouble with the church; I didn't want to get sent to prison. So I got back into doing punters, going down to the Dilly and Earls Court. I introduced Lee to it. I could not believe it, there he was a few years older than me, knowing everything; and I showed him how to do punters.

In those days I thought I was really happy. We lived in a squat with no electric or hot water. I had the life I'd always wanted: living as a prostitute, getting ultra-violet pissed, loads of money, loads of sex. I bleached my hair and had this Boy London silk jacket. I used to wear mascara and foundation. I knew I was under age, but that was a bonus. I was in demand. I was very loud and was screaming my tits off all over the place.

While it lasted, Anna and I had a fab relationship. We split up after a few weeks because she got too jealous of the other guys. We all had to move out the squat and I ended up in 'cardboard city' underneath the arches. I met this guy Madser, who took care of me. I went around with him and his girlfriend for a little while. Some dirty old hairy bastard, with clinkers all over his beard tried to force me into his cardboard box and have his way with me. Madser saved me from him: I would have been dead meat.

While I was living on the streets, my feet and trainers really stank. I wore the same trainers day in and day out. There's this guy, he drives round the Dilly all of the time, he likes big smelly trainers. He loved me! I got in his car, and we'd drive up behind the Ritz. He'd ask me to take off my trainers for him. Every time he touched my trainer he would gasp, and make a weird noise. Then he'd ask me to take my sock off. He would sniff my really smelly sock. While he was sniffing these, he wanked himself off in the car. That was it. Most of the boys have done him. That was an easy £45.

A former MP, he picks up with his boyfriend. He's well known. He often picks up boys in pairs, but this time, he picked up just me. That was when money was really bad for me. He got me pretty stoned before he caned me. He was disgusting, it was painful. He'd got loads of toys for hitting people with: canes, badminton rackets, baseball bat, cricket bat, slippers. Before you go in this room, you'd have to say, sorry, I've been naughty. He'd say, right, you are going to get fifty of these before you go into the room. Then you'll get ten of this and ten of that and so on. Then he really laid into you, I had great big weals all over me. Then he'll look at you and say, you are not laughing at me boy? Then you'd have to wank him. Then he goes out the room and his boyfriend comes in, he's a lot worse. I'd have to have a wank with him. All that for £40. It was fuck all at the time, I was quite pissed off.

I went back to my mum's shortly after that for my sixteenth birthday. She was glad to see me. My relationship with her was getting better. I still wasn't able to trust her; I couldn't trust adults for a long time to come. It was nice to have a bed and loads of home cooking. Then back to London after a few days, to the underground car park or as a sex slave at some punter's.

Juliette introduced me to this girl, Jane. She was a dancer at Heaven. She got me into drugs. I took an acid trip. I was off my tits. I went all tingly, my fingers went numb. My hands were in a cold sweat and went green. The lasers were going, the music was fantastic. I used to really bitch off at people. I was really loud. It was brilliant. I started doing loads of trips then. Jane got me into Heaven for nothing. I didn't pick up punters there; but I ripped loads off.

I was in the Star Bar and Jane would sit on the stool. Punters would follow me into the toilet and pay me. Then Jane would come and get me out. If the punters said anything, I'd say I'd get them thrown out.

Heaven was wild. All these muscly men and oily chests. I really got into dancing and performing on the stage and on the podium. I was always so off my tits on acid. Lee was like some exotic dancer.

I'd been hanging around with this guy Dave on the Dilly. A guy we knew pulled up to us in his car and said, 'I'm off to Amsterdam, there's brothels there, do you want to come?' We just had to go.

We got to Amsterdam, changed our money, booked into a hotel. We found the So What bar. It was the smartest brothel around. The manager knew Dave and gave him a job. He said I was too young, and to go across the road to the Boys Club 21. I worked there for a short while. I used to go to the So What a lot because I got to know a lot of the boys there. The owner got the hots for me. He said, 'You can go out with me, you can live with me and you can work here.' I was in love again.

At the club, I'd wander around and pick up a punter. I'd take him to the desk, ask for a room and get him to pay and I'd take him to the room. I'd get half the money. They used to stick my money in the safe. I had loads of money. More money than I knew what to do with. I was doing more punters than anyone there. I was doing six or seven punters a night. I was making more money than any boy in that brothel.

Sexually I'd do everything except fisting. Whatever they wanted. I had to tie up this guy and torture him. I got the toilet brush, kept hitting him with it and shoving it up his bum, and peed in his mouth.

They had an S&M loft upstairs. I had such a funny experience up there. I had to spank this English guy and he had a glass eye: he was bending over, he turned round and said I've got to take his glass eye out! I went hysterical – no, no, no. You can't do that, I thought that it would leave a big hole. I thought someone had set me up. I ran downstairs, I was screaming my tits off.

There was the first time I'd ever seen a pumped-up dick. His penis was that big. I seen him coming into the brothel, and I said, 'Is that your dick?' and he said 'Yes'. I pulled it out and I just had to have him. I did him and that set me off onto big dicks. I turned into a size queen. He couldn't get it hard. It was like a big lump of salami. The things I let him do to me.

In the S&M room they had this weird thing. It's like a bed and you lie on it and it vibrates. You put oil over your punter, you are supposed to get off on it. They had a sauna there. I enjoyed doing the saunas and the S&M room because you got more money. The S&M room was 375 guilders for an hour and a half, the sauna was 300 guilders. I'd get half. There were condoms around but we didn't use them. Other brothels didn't usually provide them. The punters did not want to use condoms. Who was I to say no?

Almost from day one I was into speed, E's, everything, totally drug-fucked. I got into E's bad, I felt so in love with myself. I was doing drugs first thing in the morning right through the day, every day. All my money went on drugs and clothes. After a few weeks we all got the sack from the brothel because of the drugs. My time in Amsterdam, I was at my peak. I couldn't have had any more fun if I'd tried. I wish it could have lasted longer.

I came back on to the Dilly. I met an outreach worker from Streetwise Youth. He was buying burgers for all the boys, he gave out condoms, talked about safer sex and he seemed OK. The boys said he was OK and so I went up to Streetwise. They helped me with appointments for housing and whatever, but I was usually too drug-fucked to do anything. I was doing E's and whatever all the time. I spent my nights going out to raves or wherever.

The police caught me with a punter. A punter had beckoned me over. I followed him over to the Regent Palace Hotel and he started talking to me. He asked me to go to the Piano Bar to sort out business. The next thing I knew, I was nicked for importuning. The coppers told the punter to move it and not to come back again. So the police are in on it as well, protecting the punters! Streetwise came to court to give me some support.

I went home that Christmas for a few days. I came back and started working behind the bar at the Craven Club. I was working and doing punters there. This guy Steve came in and brought me a drink. I was told he was a big time drug dealer. He said, why don't I come back and get off my face. So I did. I was there for months.

Most of the time god knows what drugs I was taking: everything. I'd open my mouth and take them just like sweets. I was off my head all the time, totally. I had no idea whether I was in a relationship with Steve. I was off my face for days, I remember wandering around in a daze saying to him, 'I'm coming down, I'm coming down, more drugs!' Then I started going to Shaftesbury's. I started selling trips for Steve. Then I fell out with him. He wanted money off me for bills.

Mikey, a rent boy, who was also staying at Steve's, said he was moving to Simon's in Earls Court. Lee and I were mates again. We moved into Simon's as well.

We were there some time. That's where I got into the smack. It was Mikey who said, 'Do you want to try some gear?' I said, 'What's gear?' I had to have some, everyone else was doing it. I chased it. As it goes, it was just what I wanted at the time. It made me feel that I had no problems in the world. Mikey was dealing it, and so it was always there. I was doing punters and making a fortune just round the block. I had Simon's dog and would walk up Lillie Road with it. Everyone would say, 'What a nice dog': I'd say, 'Do you want to come back to mine?' I made a fortune. I ended up paying for all the gear for everyone. I'd go up to Streetwise and steal food, tins of coffee, tuna, dressing gowns and flog them to pay for the gear. I got caught and barred for ages. That was one of my big problems.

I had warts on my penis, up my bum, gonorrhoea and crabs. I never got it together to get to the clinic. I was doing ten, twelve punters a day to pay for the gear. About two months later, and still sixteen, I thought, 'Fuck this, everyone's taking the piss. I'm making all the money for everyone for drugs. I'm getting off the gear and going to Amsterdam.' I rang the So What bar and they said they would give me my old job back; I was a big earner for them. I'd got a bit of money saved under the sink, I sorted my passport and coach ticket from Victoria coach station, and off I went. I remember some girl sat next to me and I told her I was getting a job in a coffee shop.

I was making a fortune at the brothel, and saving money. They treated me well because I'd been out with the owner. I started to have a fling with one of the guys there who was living with a female prostitute. I went to see them a few times. They did smack. I done a bit: I was so ill, it was too strong. I was vomiting, nothing like the smack over here, and I just stopped it. I got back into E's again.

A couple of weeks later, the owner of the Boys Parade over the road come in and said that there was an English boy over there. I went over and I couldn't believe it; it was Pete. We knew each other on the Dilly. We were already quite friendly. We got really close. He went to work in Boys Parade and we used to meet up every night. They wouldn't take him on where I was working, which was a better brothel, because he wasn't 'our sort of boy', he wasn't up-market enough. Pete met lots of other young Welsh guys at his brothel who'd been recruited by the brothel owner at Cardiff bus station. They'd been promised loads of money and work, they'd get them their tickets and passports. When the boys got to the brothel, the owner would keep hold of their passports.

In my brothel there were panic buttons if there was any trouble, which there rarely was; it was mostly local punters and regulars. In other places there was loads of trouble, no central heating, and they wouldn't change the sheets between punters, so there were stains all over the place. I never had any trouble.

I'd buy four or five E's in the morning, and I'd be constantly off my tits all day. I'd do at least six or seven punters in the day. Then me and Pete would have a real fun time. We'd try and get off work by midnight and meet in the coffee shop. I would buy ten ready-rolled spliffs for the night. We'd sometimes go into the straight sex cinema next door and watch straight blue films. They used to get soldiers in there and we'd 'play' with them: toss them off. Then we'd go on to a leather bar, and we'd run into the dark room, screaming for fun. We used to get some really nice guys in there. I couldn't get enough of it. Then we'd go on to the night sauna. The heat would bring us right up on the E's. We'd have more sex. Clean our skin out and sweat the E's out of us.

We'd then go back to the coffee shop and get some toasties, chocolate drink and spliff. Then we'd fall asleep in my brothel's cinema, watching the sex videos. I'd get up a couple of hours later and get some more E's. The day would start all over. Those E's were really wonderful for sex, I was coming maybe eleven times a day.

I couldn't handle that now. Amsterdam was nothing but sex and drugs, drugs and sex, every day. It was fab.

I wouldn't have changed any of that. It was like a dream come true. I'd always wanted it, and, when I got it, it was a hundred times better. I just love men. You could do anything. Pete was the same, he was into the same things. We got really close. He said to me, 'Whatever you do, don't leave me.' We started making a bond between us. We started having loads of threesomes. I used to talk about anything with him.

I remember ringing up my mum. Bill answered the phone and said she'd gone away with a new boyfriend on holiday. It really freaked me out. It really screwed me up. I was hysterical. I told Pete about it and he said, 'At least you've got a mum and she cares for you. My mum and dad won't have me.' When we used to come down off the E's, we used to get so depressed and we'd let it all out with each other. We were good for each other. It was what we needed at the time. We were both sixteen, and country boys from Wales. We had a lot in common. He was one of the very few people who ever knew my ways and what made me tick.

All of the boys had to go for regular check-ups for VD. Then there was another doctor who we had to see for an HIV test in his flat. There was something funny about that arrangement. We had to get these cards saying that we were all clear before we could go back to work. I got called in for the results by the brothel owner, and he said to me, 'You and a few other boys have the big "A".' That's what they called it. 'If you shut up about it, you can carry on working here. But if you leave here and try to go to another club, we'll tell all the other clubs that you are positive.'

We couldn't get any work anywhere else in Amsterdam. He wouldn't tell me what other boys had it. A few boys said he was lying about the HIV, they were just trying to keep us there. Looking back on it now, I can see the whole set-up of the HIV test was bullshit.

I was so stoned. I believed what everyone told me. I got so drug-fucked; all I could think about was, what if I can't work? I can't get money. I blocked the HIV out, but it did use to get to me. Pete had already been diagnosed in England. It was a big thing. If it wasn't for the drugs, we would have been seriously fucked up.

The last day I was working at the brothel I'd done seven rooms; made a nice lot of money. I went and bought loads of things like duvets and nice things for where I was now living. I phoned into work next day and got told that everyone had got the sack for drugs. There were thirty-five boys in the brothel for two shifts: 12 noon to 7.00 pm and 7.00 pm to 2.00 am. I was dumbstruck because I'd earned a fortune the day before and spent it all. All the boys met up in the coffee shop outside, and we put superglue on the lock on the shutters, so they couldn't close it.

Through some punters, Pete and me had heard about this place Hollywood, a brothel, in Düsseldorf. We decided to go to Germany.

We arrived there first thing in the morning. We were tired and hungry. We'd spent all our money on our fares. We hadn't eaten for three days. We had just enough to buy a salami roll between us. We were like gannets.

It was awful when we got to the brothel. We walked in there. There were fifteen to twenty boys, and they were real bitches towards us. Really bitching us. We were really uncomfortable and we didn't make any money. We were really pissed off.

We said to the manager that we were leaving. He said that the guy who owns this brothel owns four others. He rang up the one in Cologne and the guy who owned all the brothels sent a car to take us there.

We got there, it was quite late, about ten o'clock in the evening. It was gorgeous. They gave us a beer each. It was in a block of posh flats. The top floor was the brothel and the floor below was the apartments for the boys who did not live locally. We said to them that we hadn't eaten, they gave us an advance. We ordered pizza. We lived on pizza and lasagne and McDonald's.

A guy called Vladimir from Romania was running it. He was a bastard. He had some scam where he would 'employ' Romanian refugee boys and girls. He fooled the officials. He had us all good and proper. It was like being at boarding school. We had to get upstairs to the brothel about three hours before it opened to clean up from the parties from the night before. We had to wash all the glasses. Then about twelve o'clock punters would start coming. We'd finish about one or two o'clock in the morning and go out to this café. We'd go there, have something to eat, have a drink and go back to the brothel and then get woken up again in the morning. That was it. We got into the swing of things, and started to get a lot of punters and to get a load of money.

I saved up quite a bit of money. We used to go back and forth to Amsterdam to get drugs and sell them. I then discovered that Vladimir was a cokehead. There was a square bar in the middle of this huge room. I'd see him go down beneath the bar, thinking he was in the fridge getting ice. But then when he came up, he was all red, smiling, and we discovered he was on coke.

Then he told us about the drug dealer downstairs. I discovered he was selling smack, coke, speed: then all my savings disappeared. I then had a big falling-out with Pete. I got quite addicted to the coke; I was like a kid with sweets. Pete and I would agree to pay half each, but I would take most of it. I was a real bitch. I don't know how he put up with me. I was evil. I was always off my tits.

The German punters were bastards. When we were in Amsterdam and the German punters came over, you could take liberties with them. Because you were in Germany, they used to take the piss. You had to stay in the room for an hour and a half with them. They'd make you stay in the room even if they'd come. You'd have to stay there for the rest of the time. There was mirrored ceilings in the rooms, we found out they had cameras there.

Me and Pete got this German punter, we started doing him regularly. He used to think we were Welsh brothers and he used to get off on it. He'd come in three or four times a week and do us. He told Pete to fuck me, then me to fuck Pete; but we didn't use to fuck. We used to pretend. Most punters would treat us badly; fucking would be like bang, bang, bang. We used to get 100 DM for doing a punter. If we sold drinks, we'd get a third.

I had my seventeenth birthday there. I was so depressed. I didn't have one birthday card. Pete got me a big bottle of champagne, and a few drinks. I was well pissed, but well depressed.

By this time we were looking awful. We were doing too much coke and smack. We weren't getting many punters. I went four days without a punter. I was really pissed off. We had enough money to go back to Amsterdam. We got the train there. We'd been in Cologne just a few weeks.

In Amsterdam, we were unable to get our jobs back. We went to this cheap brothel. It was coming up to winter, they had no heating, and it was freezing. We made no money there. In the end we decided we'd had enough. We decided we wanted to go back to England. We had enough to get to the Hook of Holland. We thought the English there would help us get back to England.

We were starving, depressed, and suffering from withdrawal from the drugs. On the train to the Hook, we went through the bins to see if there was any food. Pete went one way: I went the other. We found a sandwich and a half between us. We were like savages. My stomach felt so awful. Pete and I made a pact never to tell anyone about raiding the bins, we were so ashamed. Pete kept going on about our HIV, and then he had me thinking about it. I had diarrhoea, all my knickers were shitty, and I thought I was going to die.

None of the English would help us with our fares. In the end we reversed the charges to a punter in England, and he got someone in Amsterdam to come down and pay our fares home.

I got back to London, stayed at various places. That was shit. I went back to my mum's for Christmas. I went back to Neath and it was hell. My mum didn't really want me there because of my peroxide hair. My prostitute auntie really slagged me off and told everyone I was on the game. My nan gave me loads of attitude on the phone and didn't want to know me. But I didn't care. I wasn't ashamed of it.

I came back to London and had a same-day HIV test. All the punters thought I was too young to have HIV, and I believed that as well, even though Pete had it. I was so sure I didn't have it.

I had a big fall-out with Pete. He said, 'I'm going to give you the best bit of advice I'm ever going to give you. Don't have your test.' He refused to come with me for the results. I went to the hospital for my results. I was the last person to be called. She hadn't even closed the door when she told me I was positive. I was dumbstruck, devastated.

She said I'd have to come back for counselling in a few days' time, no mention about what I was going to do that night.

I had nowhere to go. I needed somewhere to put my head down. I didn't know of anywhere. I ended up going back to Wapping to Steve the drug dealer's. They said, 'Welcome to the clan! We're all HIV.' I took two trips and got off my tits. Next day when I came down, I was dreadful, hysterical. I went up to Streetwise, I spent the day there crying about everything. They could find no emergency accommodation available anywhere. I wanted to go back to my mum's, I rang her, and they found the money for my fare home.

I went down there and took the whole lot out on her. I told her that none of this would have happened if she'd loved me. She shouldn't have given me the fare to come to London in the first place. She couldn't handle me or my diagnosis. She was horrified about HIV and didn't know anything about it. I had to leave.

I went back to London hysterical. I was admitted to an AIDS ward in a hospital. That was a nightmare time. I could have topped myself. I was kept under sedation. My mum came down to visit me, but there were huge dramas. There was still no emergency housing available anywhere for me. Pete wasn't around and I didn't know anywhere else to go. I couldn't cope with queuing for hours, filling in complicated forms, or getting evidence of proof for this and that, that's why I didn't go to the council. I discharged myself after a few days and went back to drug dealer Steve's again.

I started doing loads of drugs again. There were a whole lot of people staying there. They were sick: they treated me like a sex slave. At the time I didn't really realize what was happening to me. I stayed there for a couple of months, did punters. I was incapable of doing anything to sort myself out. I had no energy or concentration. I was in crisis.

Eventually I got it together to go with a worker to the council. I got myself emergency accommodation, a really good flat near Paddington. After a long time and a lot of hassle, I also got my social security.

I drifted through the next couple of years in a haze: doing punters, drugs, and various people coming in and out of my life. I don't know where those years went. I had a few relationships. I wouldn't go to the hospital, because it reminded me about the HIV, which I'd blocked out. I hate hospitals anyway; a lot of the doctors intimidate me.

I was at Bangs one evening, I was on either a trip or alcohol. There were some women from Benetton, spread out around the crowd. They come up to me and asked me if I'd ever thought of doing modelling work. I thought they were taking the piss. I was really embarrassed. I said no. They were asking me my height, my age, all of this crap. They gave me a number and I had to ring them the following Tuesday. I made sure I kept off the drugs. I met up at this place as arranged and seen this guy and woman.

They said I had to drink two litres of water a day to clear my spots. I had to get my teeth sorted out. They said that I'd be no good for photos, but I'd be good for the catwalk. I've got such a complex about the way I walk, I knew I couldn't do it. That was what fucked it up. I just didn't have the confidence. It was nice while it lasted, it made me feel better than everyone else. A two-minute wonder!

I was in Harpo's with a friend one night. We picked up this guy, Trevor, and we went back to his place. It was just up the road. This guy was loaded with money. We listened to music and took loads of coke and Special K [the drug ketamine]. He took us to a new club, Aurora, at a film studio. Fucking hell, I was off my head.

We got taken to the VIP bar. I was rolling and smoking a spliff when this guy come up and asked for some. I said no. Then my friend said, fucking hell, he's a very famous singer. I was in a world of my own. All I could think about was smoking this spliff before everyone else. Trevor was a friend of this singer. We got talking to his crowd. It finished quite early in the morning. Then we all went back to Trevor's. We had a party! They had dick pumps and everything up in the jacuzzi. There was other famous people there. Some were in the jacuzzi fucking. Everyone was shagging everyone. Everyone was doing drugs. It was fab. Everyone was totally fucked.

Trevor was well into me. He invited us to this other party, in the middle of nowhere, at this huge house. You just walked in and jumped on the bed with whoever was there. Then you'd move on into the other bedrooms. There were loads of drugs there.

I slept with everyone! We all stayed there at this huge place. Me and my friend were in bed with this famous person. There was some penis on him. I didn't really know just how famous and well known he was until afterwards. He's a very good friend of the famous singer from the last party, who was there as well. All of us were drug-fucked. All we wanted was more drugs. I was so embarrassed sniffing all this stuff and there was blood all running down my nose. I was doing loads of Special K, the amounts they had of it! I was sniffing it: having blackouts, I'd come round a bit, and then I'd fly back off, and so on.

We all had unsafe sex. Nobody could find a rubber in that room, I'm telling you. You talk about orgies! That was one hot fucking party. That was my taste of fun, the high life.

Me and Pete spent a whole summer up on Hampstead Heath. We were up there day and night. I was addicted to it, it was like a drug. I would wake up, I'd have nothing to do and so I thought I might as well go up the Heath. Loads of guys up there; married guys in the day, and mostly gay at night. You get all sorts up there: you get women up there, I seen one husband and wife up there; I thought that was shocking.

We used to make fires and bring spliff and lagers up there. We just partied with a personal stereo with some speakers. We'd be up there for hours, from one afternoon right through to the following morning, constantly having sex, mostly unsafe.

You can tell married men, most of them were so desperate they would do whatever you tell them. Most of them would have unsafe sex as well. They were all freebies. I used to get off with some dogs [not the animal kind] up there. I used to pickpocket as well. Otherwise, when I was skint, I'd go home and do a punter, get some spliff, and go back up there. Sex, sex, sex, my god that's all my life was. I stopped going up there when I started seeing some guy.

Most punters wanted unsafe sex. I think most of them thought I was too young to have anything to catch. Hardly any boyfriends wanted to use rubbers. The odd one or two would say safe sex the first time, and then you meet them again, and there's no mention of a rubber. I prefer it without a rubber. It's difficult to get turned on by punters, so it's better without. I don't really give a fuck. It's too late now. Nobody protected me when I was young, that's how I caught it. Neither did anyone tell me about it, until it was too late. If they want to risk it, let them. It may sound really bad, but that's how I feel.

Pete had a regular punter called Dick. We went to Pete's place and had a threesome, I got about £60. We arranged another threesome but Pete couldn't be bothered and so I done him myself and gave him my phone number. Pete was starting to get quite ill with his HIV. I kept Dick as a punter. All he kept on about was how he was in love with Pete. His conversations with me were all about Pete. When he had sex he would call Pete's name.

I was twenty when Pete got very seriously ill with a cancer. He was out of London, in a hospital having chemotherapy and radiotherapy and by this time had worked out a relationship with his parents and was back at home.

Dick then started coming on strong with me. He's a rich businessman in East Anglia. Mid-fifties in age, separated from his wife, really ugly and hairy. Horrible teeth, he looks like Bugs Bunny. He's got a really awful old man's penis. He's a very lonely man. I find him repulsive. It was a punter relationship that went out of control. I got greedy and I wanted more money. He wanted to get close to me, and so I thought the closer I let him get to me, the more money I could get. He wanted all this 'lover' thing: to have this super relationship, me to get a part-time job and do the cooking, milk him, and meet his friends and family. He wants to run my life. He's just a first-class paedophile, a lonely old man, always talking about young boys and always picking them up on the Dilly.

When Pete died, I became very withdrawn and depressed. I became a recluse, never went out, just smoking spliff all day. Dick would come down and see me two or three times a week with money which kept me in spliff and the odd bit of smack when I was really down. I didn't have to do any punters. I was very vulnerable at the time and Dick was very comforting, I thought maybe I'd got him wrong because he was an active member of the church. He started talking a lot about the Bible. It was what I needed at the time. I thought surely he must be a nice man. Even though he kept calling me Pete and telling me how he wanted to fuck him when he was on his deathbed.

He rang me at least three times every day and wrote every day. He was brainwashing me. It suddenly sunk in a few months later how, by cleverly using his money and the church, he had got to know a lot about me. He kept on about this fantastic relationship we were having. He kept on about planning my funeral. I think he's got something about dying boys. Then I noticed he kept talking about my younger brother, and the alarm bells started to ring.

He's very sly with his money, and started playing loads of games with me to get it. It's really out of laziness I haven't done anything. He's become very hard work. But the bills keep getting paid, and now he's paying me well over a hundred a week, plus the odd grand. I cope with him by just thinking about the money. I spend a lot of time scheming ways to get more money out of him, which I usually get. It's always exciting whether he's going to suss my schemes. The times I've told him to fuck off, before he even gets in the door, when he's driven sometimes hundreds of miles to see me. He still keeps coming back and tells me he loves me. He still keeps giving me loads of money. He's pathetic. I get such a buzz out of it.

I look back at my time in London and think that all drugs fuck you up. It makes me laugh when they say spliff doesn't: I'm a living example of what it does. It's something that makes you think you are feeling really good, but it's shit. Drugs helped me in the beginning. I couldn't have coped without them. You can block everything out, but in the end they catch up with you and put you through the most awful head-fuck, paranoia and make you really ill.

When I first started doing punters, I had a lot of trouble. God, I'd feel like heaving with most of them, they were so nasty. I then started doing E's, and then sex with anyone was fab. I'd be off my head, with loads of money, hardly remembering who I'd done.

Drugs helped me cope with hating myself and missing home. In the end my body couldn't handle all the drugs: they've fucked up my head mentally, and I felt ill every day for ages. I know it's all in my head. I've thought many times I'm going mad.

I'm dead against prostitution. I got into it because I thought sex was about love, and underneath it all I was looking for a dad. I found out who my dad was a few months ago, he won't have anything to do with me. It's done me no good mentally. A few years ago I thought it was a good way to make money, but it's not worth the price. I've lost all respect for myself for doing it. I wouldn't recommend it to anyone.

Punters are all ages, twenties to eighties, office people, city people, plumbers, the lot. It doesn't matter who they are: they are just a bunch of paedophiles. They are a load of lonely men. The younger you are, the more they want you. Forget it when you are past your sell-by date. They treat young boys like pieces of meat, just to get their rocks off. They don't think we are worth anything. I've met quite a few who just get off on going with prostitutes, just the fact that they are paying for it. They feel that they've bought you and that they can do anything with your body. That fucked me up. Yet in the end money was more important to me than my body.

Throughout my time on the streets, since I was fourteen, I was vulnerable. Punters make out they want to help you. They invite you to live with them for nothing, to get you a job or keep you. Basically, all they want is for you to be on call, a sex slave, it's much cheaper that way. It's not in their interests to really help you, is it? Otherwise there wouldn't be any boys for them to pick up!

I got beaten up a lot of times. I was forced to have sex and I was ripped off. People had sex with me while I was asleep, I was abused loads of times.

There were several times after I left home when I felt suicidal: the first few days in Paddington station were awful, if I'd had something there to do it with, I would have done. I felt so unloved and unable to trust anyone and let down by my mum.

I felt awful when I came back with Pete from Amsterdam, I was so ill, I thought the end had come. Then when I found out about my

HIV for sure, I felt like topping myself loads of times. I've got this far because I had Pete with me. He was going through the same thing. Then when he went, I felt so alone, that no one really knew what I was going through. Quite a few times I've thought that I may as well go now, rather than have all the shit later.

Streetwise played a big part in my life. It was a safe place to go. It had fuck all to do with social services or the police, which was important after all the trouble I'd had with them as a kid. It was like a home. I used it for eating, washing, phone calls, health problems, counselling, everything. I would have been dead many times over. It took time but I learned to trust them.

Out there, it was a very lonely life. I didn't have any proper friends except Pete. Not ones you could trust. They were all punters, prostitutes, drug users and out for what they could get. They all bitched about you behind your back. When I became a recluse, after Pete died, I had time to think. I had to get out of London. I was going nowhere except to an early grave.

A year ago my health started deteriorating. I have been sorting out my relationships out with my mum, my brother – who I adore – and Bill. I have been spending longer periods of time at home, and have now moved back in with them. We have our huge ups and downs but I know my mother loves me now. My nan and I have made things up. I now know this is where I belong. I have been sorting myself out. I'm getting there! I'm fit and healthy, and more or less off all the drugs. I'm looking really good. The best advice I'd give to any young boy is, 'Don't come to London.'

RIP: Paul was at home with his mum when he died in 1995.

'Simon/Simone'

'Hello.' ... 'Where're you phoning from?' ... 'Woolwich.' ... 'Oh yeah.'
... 'Have you been with a transsexual massage before?' ... 'You have.' ...
. I'm based in Catford; my name's Pearl, I'm nineteen, and half Brazilian
and half English. I've olive skin, green eyes, shoulder-length auburn hair.
Measurements are 36C, 26, 36. I'm five feet seven tall and I'm pre-operative.
I'm eight and a half inches down below; full working order, very beautiful
and very convincing. Fees start at forty and end at ninety. Anything goes,
so long as it's safe. All right?' ... 'Yeah, the eight and a half is genuine.' ...
'No, I'm not circumcised. I'm not Jewish.' ... 'No, of course not, no, no, no.'
... 'You've only got five and a half inches, that's no problem. I do O and A.
What's your name?' ... 'Right Alan, when would you like to call?' ... 'Yeah,
now: that's no problem. If you'd like to make your way to me, give me a
call when you are in Catford, then I can distinguish if you are genuine and
I'll give you the address.' ... 'All right, Alan, look forward to seeing you.'

I think prostitution is camp! You get these dirty bastards who want
to come round and see a girl with a willy and shove it in their mouth
and give you ninety quid. I cope with it, because I'm getting paid, the
power is one of the biggest thrills. It's powerful: they come here into my
room to pay me. I have the power in that room. I have what I want, I
make them do what I want. Basically, what they all want is to be dominated by a 'chick with a dick'. Oh yeah, you feel dirty, you don't want
them touching you. But you just think, *money*. It's an easy way to make
money. It's the buzz. That's the only reason I'm here. I wouldn't be here
otherwise. I can earn more money in a day than most do in a week.

I've had a couple of punters that are bi. The rest find it easier to come to a transsexual, it's easier to justify in their minds that they've gone with someone feminine. It's easier for them to go with a tranny than a man-man. Most are just basically gay. The first thing they do is tell you that they are straight and then, before you know it, they're down on your nosh and come back up after five minutes for a breath of fresh air. It's just the willy they're after, not the girly things about you. Ten per cent might like the stockings and suspenders, but ultimately, they want to be dominated, held down. Then they want you to screw them. They are not into your tits. I think to myself, does it leave me feeling very masculine? I answer to myself, no, because I feel like the most dominant bitch on earth.

Most punters are nasty-looking, they are no one you'd even glance at. Even when they just touch you or kiss your body, you just think, ugh – you just want to scrub yourself out. You know, if you've got someone repulsive looking and doing you, it makes you feel nasty. Then there's the after-effects, it's all the wet on my bum, I don't like that feeling. I'm left to feel whatever ... I don't like the feeling, just like the feelings I got as a kid from my abuse.

You do get a few that are good-looking, or even decent, or you get someone who's human, that's a bit different. But you can't get attached or get involved. I've had many come back to me, good regulars, you give them the honest biz.

I've only ever had one humorous punter. That was, 'Yes, mistress, no, mistress', I had to dominate and drag him round the flat. I just found that humorous. He was wearing just his socks. I just dragged him around and told him he was dirty; said he was naughty and he had to do what I told him. Then he'd say, 'Is that good enough? Yes, mistress, no mistress.' That's the only humorous one I've ever done. None of them make me laugh.

Some want love and affection; about ten per cent. They kiss you and go the whole way. They come back and see me. They do; because they like me. They don't know you as a person, but they like you, respect you and come back. That's OK. A man earlier today was really sweet, even though he was an old hog, dressed in his city suit; he bought me a bottle of vodka. Some are nice, they tell you they love you, that you are pretty, they say nice things about you. Afterwards, I feel angry with them. I say, 'Where are you going now?' and they say they are going back to the wife. That gets me very angry. It makes me think, how can they do that to their wives? Come round here and go with a transsexual, their wives haven't a clue. There's only been a couple who feel genuine. I think they could be happy with a transsexual. Only a couple.

It's rare a man comes in here with a suit and a tie. For a lot of them it's a lot of money for them to fork out. Many of them are people in travelling jobs, builders and tradesmen.

This last punter that I've just done; he was coming on sixty, born in Amsterdam, very liberal, charming, nothing was an issue. What was an issue for me, was that he said, 'Don't have that operation. You are not going to have it, are you? You don't need it.' He said, 'Look at your body. You are just every inch a woman.' He was just amazed by me. He said, 'Don't have that operation: that'll finish you.' It was good, coming from him.

I'm not one for saying I want a sex change, because I don't know what it would be like to have a vagina between my legs; I wasn't born with one. It's ultimately the woman's body I want: the girly appearance and to be accepted as Simone. Downstairs is fine as it is. I'm confused with downstairs but I'd be even more confused with a vagina put there. I don't think that having the sex-change operation at this time in life will alter anything there is about my appearance. I'm quite happy with that now. I'm transsexual, not a woman, I can never be a real woman, not even with a vagina put there.

I'm not able to come. I get the feeling of it, but nothing will come out. It's not frustration, it doesn't matter, the hormones switch off whatever it is in there anyway. So, you're lucky, you're not left feeling frustrated: you're contented. I'm not into fucking. Although I've recently surprised myself and broken my virginity with Ken, my boyfriend. When I came off the hormones, before I had my breasts done, it wouldn't stop going up. Now I've been back on them since the operation, it takes a while

95

for it to go up. The hormones cut out that frustration in your brain, so you are not left feeling, oh my god, I've got to come. You're contented. A gamble on having the operation is whether afterwards you are left with having any sexual feelings or not downstairs. It's not important as I don't like sex anyhow, and I'm not really interested in downstairs.

When I'm about thirty and retired, maybe I'll go and get it done. I see myself being famous. Lots and lots of money for being Simone. If this waif look goes out, I can see myself going on the catwalk: 'Simone transsexual'. It's just glamorous, to have everyone looking at me. I always wanted to be an air stewardess when I was a kid. To go up and down the aisle having people looking at me. Getting attention, knowing that they'll know I've got a cock between my legs. I've given that up because now I've had my implants, and they'll blow up when I go on the plane. I could always work on a boat, I suppose: cruising!

I think my transsexuality is linked to my childhood sexual abuse. It's something I'll never know for sure. The doctors have their rights for theories, because they've got their diplomas. It doesn't mean they've always got the right answers. The doctors say transsexuality is in you from the age of four, which I don't believe. What I do know and feel about me doesn't fit in with their theories. I don't think it's something any doctor's got a right to tell me, after the sexual abuse I've been through, that his theory is right; that I was transsexual from the age of four and it was already in me.

Maybe that's why I can't understand what I see when I look downstairs. When I look down below, I don't understand; there's things about myself, my sexuality, I've got hang-ups about. The abuse has got to have had an effect on it. But the fact that I'm transsexual, I'm quite happy with.

There are a lot of *other* things in my life I've been very unhappy with; in fact devastated by. I've been crying out for help all my life.

I've tried to OD [overdose] about twelve times in the last nine months. I was so paranoid; I thought everyone was against me. I was full of nasty feelings. I wanted to kill my only friend Steve by hammering him to death in his sleep when he stayed round. I thought he was playing mind games with me. He was making me paranoid. Ken got me out of that.

That's when my head started going really bad. I OD'd on Valium many times. Ken would call the ambulance and I'd go to hospital.

I just thought I'd cracked up. Lost touch with reality. Nothing was going to make me happy, being caged up indoors, feeling all these nasty feelings, I just thought life weren't worth living. I was doing a lot of self-harm, cutting my arms. There were times when I cut my arms and I'd just cry. There was a point where I still cared that I didn't die. There was two of me. I didn't a hundred per cent want to die; ninety per cent to die and ten per cent to be found. There's a part of me inside that still wants to survive, but I didn't know how.

I was OD'ing regularly until I went through the bad crisis: I tried to hang myself when Ken was out. He came back and found me strung up, about to jump from the coffee table. I'd tied a rope round my neck, tied it to a knob on the top cupboard in the bedroom. The doctors got called in and then they sectioned me. I was off my trolley.

Now, for the first time in my life, I've got people around who want to help me. I've got my social worker who gives me counselling and other help, I've got my psychiatrist, my GP and Ken my boyfriend. Even so, I am paranoid about all of them.

I'm now looking back through my life to sort out my problems. I was born Simon, twenty-two years ago. There's me, my twin brother Peter and four other brothers and sisters. My dad is South African, black, and my mum is Jewish, white. My dad came over on a boat and he was one of the scrubbers on the decks. He had a nervous breakdown when he came to this country. He met my real mum and my mum's always been in this country.

I was put in care with my twin when I was three months old. My dad suffered from severe paranoid schizophrenia and my mum was leucotomized [operation on the brain] after being diagnosed paranoid schizophrenic. All of my brothers and sisters are in care. I came out of care last year: on my twenty-first birthday. Chucked out into the big wide world. For twenty-one years of my life I've been under Hackney social services' care: it was pathetic.

Me and Peter was put in a home in Woodford till we was five. My other brothers and sisters was put in different homes. My solicitor has recently found out that me and my twin was both physically really ill and in hospital for the first year there. Peter turned out brain-damaged and was backward.

Apparently, we was fostered out for trials, or people coming to have a look at us, but nobody wanted us. We was troubled kids, disturbed: that's not surprising from not being cradled. Then we got fostered out to the Fowlers where I stayed till I was fourteen.

We had a very unhappy time: subject to physical abuse and torment. My foster parents, they didn't care, both of them. They were bastards, they had their own son who was spoilt. We never had any privileges, me and my twin. We was forever getting told off for the simplest thing, I was picked on all the time. They probably fostered me for money, they said they never got a penny but of course they did. There was no love at all.

I never loved my foster parents, I used to hate them. They treated me like shit. All I ever wanted to do was be like the kids down my street, to be able to go to the fridge. Their own son was four years younger than us, he could go to the fridge and help himself to whatever. I wasn't even allowed to ask, if I did, it was just another reason to hit me. I got hit for the slightest thing. We were like servants; do the cleaning and the shopping. Do this, do that.

They were very ignorant. They had no understanding of what they wanted or I needed. I don't remember having conversations, they used to just sit me down and lecture me. He used to go on about that in his day it was this and that. Just pathetic conversations looking back. They never asked me how I felt, or what was going on in my head. In the end, I started stealing; steal from the cupboard, steal from the fridge, steal from the purse, take £20 notes. I could then go to school and buy sweets. I never had anything as a kid. The foster parents' son was spoilt with toys, clothes; us, we were put in Oxfam rags. I used to think that's not fair, like Cinderellas, me and Peter. The whole thing about their fostering was that they wanted power over two human beings. They said that they'd try to love us but my behaviour was why they could not.

Gary was the Fowlers' best friends' son. He was my only friend and comforter during these years of mental torment. He was twenty when I was five.

We was babysat by Gary's mum. We'd be taken over to their house. We'd be round there a lot of weekends, and some days in the week. We used to share Gary's room when we stayed over. It was then that he … he was very gentle, and I'd be on my front, he'd take my trousers down, and he'd be on my back. I don't think he put it in all the way, I think he put it in about half way. Then he'd pull out, and come all over my back. Then he'd rub it in my back with his peesh [slang for penis]. I was only five years old when it started.

Me and my brother, he used to have both of us one after the other, or just me. There was a relationship between me and him, more so with me than my twin. He used to take us to the parks and do it. What else he'd do was, he'd say to his mother can he take Simon upstairs to help with the hoovering or help clean up his bedroom? And then he'd stick a big wardrobe up in front of the door. So, if anyone did knock, he'd say, hold on a minute, pull my trousers up and that was it. It happened secretive. They'd never have guessed anything was going on.

When I got older, I was just put round there because I used to go chambermaiding with Gary's mum, in a hotel between the Embankment and Charing Cross. She used to take me with her and I would help her. So, I'd sleep round and sleep in his bedroom. So he'd all night to do whatever. So that's how it happened.

Twice it happened round Gary's best friend's house. His best friend done it too. When he done it, it was nasty. He pissed all over my back, at least, that's what it felt like. It might have been cum looking back, but as a kid, it felt like he pissed all over me. He was nasty. He was brutal. With him, I felt dirty, I thought it was wrong. It was the way he done it; he had no feelings. Gary must have discussed with his friend that he was abusing me. He must have discussed with him that he was getting his end away, and here – you do it too – they'd been laughing at me.

I don't think his mum suspected anything, not one bit. She couldn't've. She wouldn't let it go on, would she? I don't even know if they did know or not. That's something I will never know. Because abusers do it so slyly, it's clever how they do it. I don't think, looking back, you would suspect anything's happening. 'Cos any chance he would get, he'd grab it. And besides, we shared the room. When we were babysat, we'd be in his room.

I don't know how I felt, being a kid and that happening, because Gary never hurt me. He was my friend. It's only now as an adult, when people tell you it's wrong, then the whole of it turns round, and it becomes an issue. That's how it gets so confusing. Then you realize you've been abused. You don't know how to feel. I don't hate him. I wouldn't say I love him, but I'm still infatuated.

Society has their views of abuse. I've got my views about it. The only thing that affects me with the abuse is because of my brother. It's the only thing that makes me feel bad. It's because it has left Peter scarred. Even he tried to commit suicide a while back. I'm sure it has left me scarred, but I know that I'm a lot stronger than him. I look at the terrible scars on my arms, I never did it to kill myself. First you think, am I here? Is this really happening to me? You then cut and it's when you see the blood: it's a relief. I always look at the scars and see a mess. I'm scarred for life.

Every year social services would come and visit. When I used to complain that I was unhappy, and wanted to be moved, no one listened to me. Adults didn't listen, they think you are too young to make that sort of decision. Too young to speak the way you do. Too young to know what you know. You're just a kid. When I was a kid, I was deep and I was good at expressing how I feel. Would anybody listen? No, they wouldn't.

I was a loner. I didn't have any friends. I wasn't allowed to invite people back for tea. I just didn't fit in. I hated school. I hated the schoolboy's uniform and I hated team sport. I can't remember much, maybe that was because I was unhappy. I was *disturbing*, that's what they used to call me. I got the whole class going. I'd argue with the teachers, backchatting and being disruptive. Not doing as I was told. It used to set the other kids off. It used to get the teachers, not doing as I was told. Looking back I must have been very distressed; knowing that I was going back to my foster parents to be physically abused.

As a kid, I looked very girl/boy, very androgynous. I had my hair in a crew cut, my foster parents made me have it very short. I was very slim, skinny. I was quite underdeveloped, but had good calves because I was good at running.

At school, I was always a loner, but attention, attention, I always needed attention. I did it by just being different, pansified, just camp. No one ever bullied me. They all thought I was a nutter. Everyone used to say I was sweet. I had such a girly voice before it broke. I was short, the shortest in my class, I hated the boys' showers. As I walked past the boys, they'd clench up against the wall and say, 'Bums away', meaning 'bumboy'. I wanted the boys to look at me and get their attention but I wasn't into their bums.

I think I was twelve when I burned down half the classroom. No one was in the classroom, it was lunchtime. Everyone was out playing except me. I just wanted to set a fire. I got a Duracell battery and put it in a plastic bag with some matches and other bits and pieces. I wanted to see if the battery would go up in flames. I put the lighted match in the bag, then the bag started burning, but the battery didn't go up. Then I left it. Then suddenly the battery flared up and it got out of hand and I ran out the class. Next day, the headmaster called me up, but I denied it the whole way. I never got done for it. He couldn't prove it was me but guilt must have been written all over my face.

I can't remember much about my relationship with my twin. We were in different classes because he was backward. We were always fighting, but I still loved him. I remember one day; some boy was picking on him at the back of the playground. I could see him being picked on; he was crying. I left this boy with a bald patch: I pulled his hair out. That's how much anger I had in me. I was the dominant twin. I took care of him and looked after him. I always looked out for him. We wasn't close, close as in brothers. I think looking back I would rather've had a sister.

It all came to a head when I was fourteen. I was talking to some boy in class about sex. The teacher must have had an idea I was being sexually abused. She held me back after class. She talked to me and things came out. She found out I'd been abused, it all got out into the open and then Gary got jailed for eight years. I got the blame from my foster parents because it was their friends' son.

I had no one in the world to talk to. I thought, why are they taking him away from me? What's he done wrong? I didn't know. I wanted him back. I grieved for him. He gave me love and friendship: it was more than just doing his thing. He was a comfort throughout them years, from the torment of my foster parents. That sexual abuse was quite a comfort because he was also my friend. Without him, god knows what I would have done. He also cheered me up, was nice to me – no one else was. Once they put him away in prison, I could not understand why they put him there.

I was referred to the educational psychologist because of my behaviour. They put me in a special school, near Leyton, where all the kids were disturbed and had been expelled from other schools as well. Then I got thrown out of there. I was too bad, I was attacking staff or fighting. I didn't like men workers. They were a threat to me. Maybe 'cos I was so effeminate, that I was on the defensive and I thought they didn't like me.

I'd punch the men teachers or I'd get into arguments with them. They'd say, 'Get down to work', and I'd say, 'Don't talk to me like that', and I'd go for them. Then I'd get warnings for doing something wrong and I'd ignore the warnings and carry on. I was also doing it because I was distressed. At that time I was getting more distressed because the abuser had been put away. It was the beginnings of being even more unhappy at home. I think it all comes out in school, somehow. Especially when you see other kids disturbed and they flip. Or you see other people have a tantrum – makes you have one. Gets them feeling stirred up, 'cos you feel exactly how they do. You know how they feel. Getting churned up. You end up going. You see someone go, flip, and then you'd go and flip.

It all got too painful and I did a runner from my foster parents shortly after. I ran away. I didn't know where to go, so I ran to the police station. I told them I wasn't happy. They said I'd have to go back to the foster parents. I said *no fucking way*, I'd run away because I was very unhappy with my foster parents.

I left Peter there. I feel responsible for leaving him there, he wouldn't come, he was there for about a year after I ran away. It was my own decision after Gary went. I was then placed with an emergency foster parent and that broke down and I was moved into a care home, on review, in Dalston. I stayed there for nine months and I asked if they would put me in a therapeutic community because I'd cracked up. They put me in this private home in Margate, which was not a therapeutic community. It was a home for difficult black kids.

The place was an absolute dump. The woman who owned it was absolutely loaded. She was making huge profits off the place. She lived in a beautiful countryside house at the top of the road and she had a beautiful car. There were hardly any staff and they couldn't cope. They got beaten up and I was subject to torment because of being effeminate. I always stood up for myself. I was always fighting and arguing. In the end it all got too much and I ran away after six months. When I was picked up, social services put me into a therapeutic community nearby.

I was now sixteen. The social services didn't discuss with me what sort of community I wanted. I wanted one where I could have a lot of one-to-one counselling time to deal with my sexual abuse. Where I was placed was in a group where I had to talk about my feelings in front of everybody. I didn't want to discuss the gory details in front of the group. I had so much going on inside me, no one was helping me the way I needed; I ended up threatening the staff with knives and smashing the windows in. I ran away after four months.

I felt threatened by male workers, I thought all men were bastards: that hasn't changed much, even now. That was from being abused. I thought of them as a threat. They used to threaten me. Inside, I used to feel I just didn't like men. I didn't mind boys; I just didn't like men. I found them all to be perverts. I used to always think that there was something else going on with them. I couldn't sit and have a one-to-one with them. I'd feel very uncomfortable. Women were no problem: they used to make me feel safe, mothered and sistered. Like when I had key workers, they were always women. I used to get on with them so well. It's hard to explain; I could just sit and talk with them about the way that I felt. I couldn't, to a man. Even if I was just down; I couldn't say that to a man. I always felt that men had no emotions. They had one thing in mind and that was sex, that's all they were. That's why I was fighting and threatening them. Workers didn't want to know about my reasons why I was like that. Even now, I just want women workers.

My social worker said I was threatening and violent, and they had no other placements for me. By this time I'd actually visited my mum and dad for the first time since I'd been taken away from them. I wanted to live with them. I thought everything would be like 'Surprise Surprise!' with Cilla Black. It all ended up not to be like that.

At home, and still aged sixteen, my transsexuality started to come out. I began to realize that I wanted to be a girl. That there was something wrong. My dad wouldn't stand for it. He would put me in boys' clothes, made me have my hair cut short. I was rebelling against that. I was very unhappy. I couldn't tell him about the way I felt.

My mum, I got on really well with. I used to brush her hair, and do all nice things with her. She wasn't a problem, but I couldn't cope. I phoned my social worker on numerous occasions, she said they would not move me. I was the one who asked to go home; and home is where I should stay. So I took a big overdose of my mum's tablets; she was heavily sedated herself. I went into a coma. I was well out of it for two weeks.

I'd only been at home for just two weeks, and then out of it for two weeks following my overdose, when social services put me into a lock-up. That was in Redhill. They put me in there because they said I was a danger to myself, they put me on assessment. It was an all-boys secure unit, for young offenders. I wasn't an offender. I wasn't a criminal. But I didn't seem to realize that at the time. I felt trapped. I felt that I wasn't meant to be in this all-boys place. I'm not saying that it was appropriate to put me into an all-girls' place because that wouldn't be right. They could have put me into a mixed secure unit. In the end they let me out of there after six weeks.

I was now just seventeen and placed in another children's home in Hackney. I stayed three months. I used to go out and get cans of

Tennent's, got drunk and my hysterical feelings came out. I used to go back to the female staff and cry my eyes out. I mourned for Gary. I wanted him back. I ended up threatening the male staff.

I was then taken back to another all-boys lock-up, again on assessment, this time in Croydon. I was freaking out. I was telling them at that time that I wanted to be a girl, they said I had to wait till I was older. I said, no way am I waiting, just let me see a doctor. No, they wouldn't let me see a doctor. So that placement broke down after three months.

They decided they would send me to a place in Dorset. It was a private hospital. They gave me a brochure of the place. It looked absolutely lovely. It turned out I was put in a psychiatric behaviour unit. I was told if I were to stop the violence, stop being naughty, they would help me with my gender. That was a lie! They'd already had a meeting the previous week, before I went. I got told that they weren't going to deal with my gender, I was there for my behaviour. I had to fight the system. You had to earn your points, etc. They began to realize how I really wanted to be Simone and how severely I was transsexual.

There was a woman worker in there who I believed was a dyke; she was on my side. She gave me an article on Caroline Cossey, who sold her story, about her life as 'Tula', to the papers. She passed me the paper over. That's when I went – *that's it* – I now know. It was the first time that I realized that there was actually someone else out there like me. I thought, god, I want to be like her. It took months of persevering and fighting. I broke down those rules. In the end, I was in full-blown drag. Then they let me have the right to be Simone. I said, if you don't give me what I want I'd rather die. I was beginning to see little black hairs popping through my face and I was beginning to become masculine and that wasn't what I wanted.

The placement broke down because I threw a bowl of boiling hot custard over a member of staff's head. That was because he was bullying all the kids. He was tormenting them. I thought enough was enough. So they booted me out of the hospital. They couldn't cope with me. Which was good, because I got out of the hospital and I was on my way to being Simone.

I was still seventeen years old, in my bedsit in Tottenham, still under social services, when I heard of AIDS. I was referred to the Terrence Higgins Trust [voluntary organization providing information, education and support to those infected and affected by HIV and AIDS] for counselling. I was paranoid that I'd got it, because Gary, the actual sexual abuser, was a haemophiliac and there was a high chance he may have been infected; he'd been fucking me all those years. It was through them I decided to have the test and they also told me about the TV/TS centre [meeting place for transsexuals and transvestites, now closed down].

I was over the moon when the test came back negative.

I went down to the TV/TS centre and got some counselling and was referred to a doctor. I went to see him private, £20 at his clinic. He then referred me to the hospital clinic where he worked and he put me on hormones. If it hadn't've been for these, I would have been some hunky butch fellow.

At the centre, I met another transsexual. She later took me to a bar in Soho. After that I wandered around there on my own. Then I bumped into someone who looked really unusual and different and I stopped her. Being bitchy, I said, 'You're a man aren't you?', not realizing that she was. She went, 'No, but you are, aren't you?' I said, 'Yes I am.' She said, 'I am too.' I went in disbelief, 'No!'

Then Kay and me, we got meeting and chatting, and I ended up seeing her again. She introduced me to a club called Heaven. I met her in there. I took my first ecstasy with her. God, can I remember it! It was camp. I went round squeezing all the queens' bums and grabbing hold of their peeshes, and trying to snog them. I got boxed. They don't like that, do they! They must think I was a fag hag. I was outrageous, I really was. It was the love drug. You'd meet queens and say 'Hi', and when everyone went back to a 'chill-out' afterwards. Everyone loved everybody. You'd have friends you didn't know. 'Ooo, I love you too!'

It was Kay who told me about clipping. She told me it was easy money. I was with her and another tranny and they clipped a guy. They done £425 and split it between the three of us. I got over £100 for doing nothing. I thought, wow, this is it. Then I got into being friends with her. Then I went out and worked with her. I thought, this is the life. Better than being on £33.60 benefits. I was still trying to get my sickness benefit.

If the police can't get you for importuning, they'll get you for highway obstruction. The fines mount up at £50 a time, £30 a time and in the end they mounted up to £800. I refused to pay them. I had to go to prison four times altogether, for different fines. I actually went to Feltham, an all-boys place. Three times for not paying fines, the fourth time for a social enquiry report for importuning. The longest I was ever there was ten days. It was camp. The boys kept calling me she. I provided them with all the entertainment and they loved it. They were all whispering in my ear in the video room.

It made me laugh, because when I was in there, an all-boys place, even the screws when they do a strip search, they would turn their heads. They'd turn away and let me undress. That was one real experience.

I never got done for deception while I was clipping: I got done for importuning. If they catch a guy going up to a guy and asking for sex, they can nick you for importuning. They'd never actually caught me with a punter, but they still nicked me. Not for soliciting, because that's a woman's charge; in the eyes of the law, I'm still a fella. I got done for importuning while working as a girly.

That was embarrassing. The most embarrassing moment of my life being in the courtroom. These cute boys eyeing me up, them thinking – cor, look at her! Then the clerk come out with 'Simon——*he* has been charged with … '; you should have seen the shock horror on everybody's face. I stood there and went 'Ahem!' to the judge, 'I'm a she, actually.' He said, 'If you say that one more time, I'll do you for contempt of court.' I said, 'Well, I am a she.' He said, 'Well, in the eyes of the law you are a man.' I said, 'In the eyes of the law, I might be a man, but what do I look like?' He said, 'Enough of this.'

I looked around at the people in the court and said, 'Well what do I look like?' He said, 'Well you look like a girl, and I'm doing you for contempt of court; a £20 fine.' I also got done £50 for importuning.

I hated living on my own. I couldn't cope with the responsibility.

I was taunted by the people down the street. I hadn't been dressing as a girly for very long, I must have looked really draggy in them days: tight miniskirt, stilettos, heavy make-up, not the part I do now. I ended up homeless and living from floor to floor. I ended up every night in the clubs on the gay scene. I was meeting people and staying with queens everywhere, I moved in with Kay for a month in Earls Court and worked the streets, bringing punters back. I also worked an all-guys' agency, at that time they only had one transsexual working on the books and that was me. Then, they were very highly exclusive. You had to have that real look to get in. Now they are money grabbers, anyone they'll have. They loved me as a transsexual. All the guys had to be gorgeous. Now they look just like anorexic star brats, that need feeding up.

Every weekend for the first couple of months, I was out there grafting during the week and out at the clubs at the weekend. Then it was the clubs every day. Any excuse to go out. We'd even go to a club called Underground on a Tuesday. You've never heard of it? That's because nobody went there! Yet I'd still find my way there. Any excuse to take an ecstasy. Clubbing and taking ecstasy; that was happiness. I was getting loads of money from working.

I only ever had two bad E's, and that was because they didn't work. When I was first on the scene they cost £15 and then they went down to £10. They have all sorts of names: 'Doves', they make you lovey-dovey, they give you such a rush, they're one of the strongest and the best. They cost £15. You'd just sit there and pull faces. Just sit there wrecked, you knew you was out of it. The rush would last for about six hours constantly. You only had to take one or two, two at the most. But I'd get greedy and take three. Then there's 'Dennis the Menace', red and black capsules. Then there was the orange and green caps, then there was orange and white, there was 'Burgers', 'Yellow Burgers', 'White Burgers', then there was 'Callies' (Californian Sunrise). That's the ones I can remember.

I was eighteen when I met Neil. He was my first boyfriend, straight, he was one beautiful boy. We lasted nine months together. We stayed in a squat in the King's Road. We did the clubs together. We took E's together. He rented and I clipped to get money. He even took me to see his mum in Southampton. He was with it at one point, then he lost it. Me and him didn't last because he was totally tripping, constantly. I just wasn't getting anywhere with him.

Did you know he beat up his own mum? That put him really on a guilt trip, because he was tripping at the time. He nearly put his mum into intensive care. He did the same thing to me one night, but not that bad. Because I was his size, I could fend him off. When he came back down, he thought I was his mum. He thought I was the devil; he was freaked out and I was heart-broken. We had a fight around his house, he said, 'I think it's best we call it a day.' I said, 'I think it is as well.' I was heart-broken. I really loved that boy. Neil gave me up because he loved me. I gave him up because I loved him. If I'd stayed with him any more, he would probably have killed me. Which wasn't his fault.

Poor old Neil, he suffered: he's now dead, an overdose. It happened about five months ago. When I heard that news it traumatized me.

I heard about Streetwise when I was with Neil, he took me there. He said that they were bound to take transsexuals, and they did. I liked Streetwise; there's always staff on, and workers at night. Streetwise was very children's-home-like to me, in a way. It was the safest I'd felt in a long while. The only place I knew I could go if things got really on top. I always knew I could go to somebody I liked there, and they would sort it out.

Everything I've ever really liked has failed; everything. Some of it has been my doing. Look at Streetwise, that's a prime example. I cried when they closed. I felt like dying, I had nowhere to go for help.

They helped me get some temporary accommodation, a bedsit in Stroud Green. I didn't stay there much because of doing the clubs and E's. But after about a year or so of doing the clubs, I started getting really, sort of, paranoid, I was beginning to go edgy at clubs. I thought everybody knew I was on edge or people were conspiring to make me crack up.

I knocked it on the head when I went with Nigel, my next boyfriend. I was nineteen and a half years old. I stopped my drugs and I went off the gay scene. I stopped for about fifteen months while I was with him. The thought of drugs and clubs used to bug me for the whole time I was with him. I still wanted to do it, sort of. But the thought of going to, say, like Trade, my stomach churned and I'd have butterflies in my stomach. I couldn't go through that scene again. The thought made me so paranoid.

I met Nigel in Heaven, in a gay club, just out of the blue. I stopped working totally. He went out nicking and thieving and I lived off him. I got attached to Nigel and everything was sweet. I wanted it to be like what it was like with Neil; I didn't want a one-night stand; I didn't want to go out and sleep around. I thought this is the one for me. He knew I thought that. He knew I felt that and so I played into his hands. I was in love with him, I loved him and I cared about him.

It was hell. He made up lies, stories. He was just a bastard, basically. He beat the shit out of me. He mentally tortured me. He broke my nose. He'd fling me around, kick and spit, he was violent. He'd hold me to the floor and call me a nigger lover. He was white. Yet I loved him. Some love was better than no love at that time. He used to say, you're with me because you're frightened of being on your own. If I'd stopped to think about me, I would have been out of that relationship, long gone. I always thought, how is he going to cope if I leave him? I used to put it down to the fact that he's got problems. He was always a nasty piece of work.

One day, I was talking about the abuser [Gary] and said I thought I was still in love with him. Nigel beat me up and kicked me down the stairs and said, 'How can you be in love with the abuser, you dirty bitch, after all he's done to you?' I really thought I was in the wrong. When I realized, I was cutting my wrists and taking it out on me. That was the first ever time I ever cut myself, that was two years ago. He stood there and watched me do it. He'd pushed me over the edge. I done it in front of him, he'd made me so angry.

If I'd been with someone kind, and come out with that, he would have tried to understand or talked me through it. But you should not get beaten up for what's been done or for what you feel. The guilt [for

110

being in love with her abuser] was three times as much. How come all the transsexuals I know, all their boyfriends beat them up? It's because the boyfriends can't handle their sexuality: they are gay. They are beating them up because they should be with a man.

I know a transsexual called Linda, who is now HIV. She went through exactly what I went through, but she's been lumbered with AIDS as a goodbye present. Her boyfriend knew what he was doing. He went and slept with a guy who had AIDS and went and give it to her. He knew it was coming to an end. He used to batter her. They went out with each other for five years. Every single transsexual I know, their boyfriends beat them up. The boyfriends can't handle it because they are so fucked up. They are with them because they are transsexual, not with them because they like Simone for being the person Simone. It's easier to be with a transsexual than it is to be gay. It's wrong.

Nigel said he'd never been with a man before, but that was a lie. I found out that he'd been with a guy who's well known on the gay scene. One evil fucker – does his little rent boys. He's the work of the devil.

I was very vulnerable when I met Nigel. I needed love. I was very, very vulnerable. I was too vulnerable. If I'd been with it, I wouldn't have stood for half of what I did. I wasn't with it. That was the whole point of going through all that; just hoping that at the end of it, it would get better.

We moved to Brighton to start again. But he didn't change. While I was there, the rumour went round London that Simone had died, everyone thought I'd died. I got back in touch with Steve, who I'd met on the club scene the previous year, and I ran away to stay with him for a month back in London. I was then housed by the Homeless Persons' Unit in a special place for the vulnerable. Nigel found me and I got moved again because he got too violent.

I thought he was ill. He wasn't ill. He went to a mental hospital. Got himself sectioned. When I heard he had cut his wrists, I thought, oh my god, he's not evil; I've got it all wrong. I went round to his house and he was really shocked to see me. He never thought he would see me again. Then I brought him back here after, because I really did love him. He

111

was cuddling me and I was drifting away. I was thinking, don't touch me. All the things you have done to me, why did you do it to me? He said, 'Oh don't start', then he calmed down.

In the morning we got up at midday. He said he wanted to be with me again. I said, I need some time and space to figure this out. He wouldn't give me the space. He said, 'Let me stay here all day. I'll keep out of your way.' I said, 'Please Nigel, can you just go, you don't change do you? I'll phone you later.' So he threw me down on the bed and put his hands around my neck and said, 'I got myself sectioned, so that I can fucking kill you. I know what I'm doing.' It put the wind up me. He made out as if he was going to strangle me. He said, 'You can get off on that now: I know where you live.' He got off and left. Freaked the life out of me. Someone doing that. He knew what he was doing. Then I went on being here on my own, fearful. I wouldn't come back here at night because I was too frightened. I used to stay out in Soho clipping. I would go out late and wouldn't get back till it was light, about four or five o'clock in the morning.

Looking back he represented the abuser [Gary], the abuse, and I cared and loved him. That was what I was used to. But when I was with him at the time, I don't know what I thought. Coming out of that relationship I know has done me good. I know what I won't put up with.

Then the end phase of leaving Nigel, I was just coming up to my twenty-first birthday, I went back out on the scene and had a good binge on the E's. After I'd been out once, it wasn't as bad as I thought it would be. It was all new and exciting. I went out with Steve, who became my spiritual twin. There were times we'd go on the binge from Monday to Monday. All the clubs we'd do. You name it … Mondays we'd go Busby's, Tuesday we'd go to Substation, Wednesday was Pyramid, Thursday was Bangs, Busby's, Friday was Garage at Heaven, Saturdays was best because Saturdays was Heaven first, then Trade all-nighter, then Sundays was Villa in the day and FF club at night. It would be non-stop. With chill-outs, going round to people's houses after the clubs, in between. Weekends, I could do thirty E's. We were both doing punters to pay for them.

But soon I started feeling edgy again and paranoid. Glued, I couldn't dance and had to stomp sometimes from one side of the club to the other, trying to fight it. One night I left the club because I was paranoid and went looking for Steve. He was sitting in his friend's car and I went and sat in the car with him. I've only recently realized he was paranoid too. It just basically got worse. In the week, the clubs were fine. Heaven was fine, but as soon as it came to go to all-nighters we'd be edgy, just sit there. We'd end up leaving the clubs all the time.

I thought everyone knew I was paranoid, and that I was trying to fight it. I hoped it didn't show. In the end we'd end up leaving the clubs. We kept on doing it till I said enough's enough. Steve and me would say we're not going out for the weekends, then after a couple of months it came to a point where we just couldn't do it no more. We said we'd do E's and sit indoors, but go on to chill-outs.

Then we cut down more and we'd usually go out in the week in the day and get wrecked, walk through the cemetery and get wrecked. There were days when we had two-day binges, we cut down because there was nowhere we could go without feeling paranoid. I'd calmed down.

I was working from my flat by putting ads in the papers. One night I'd done acid with Steve and ended up having a big row. I hadn't slept properly; I'd only had two hours' sleep. I needed money, so I went down to Soho. I was walking away from the police and met up with a couple of guys I knew. They pointed out some guy looking at me. I saw this guy across the road, looked over and thought *cor*! I was still quite paranoid at the time, but I got the two guys to go over and talk to him, and he came over and we spoke. I said, 'What are you doing?' He said he was going to go to Bloomsbury. I said, 'I'll kill time while the police go.' So I ended up going in the car with him.

In the car we had a conversation, he told me his name was Ken. It came up that his last girlfriend was a transsexual, so I knew I had no worries in saying, well – I'm a fella. So that eased the ice. After he'd done whatever in Bloomsbury, we ended up going to Substation together, and then he came back here with me. We stayed together that Saturday and all day Sunday and he left in the evening saying he was going to write to me. He sent me a card and things started rolling from there.

He moved in four weeks after we met in October last year, then I started losing track. Ken says I started OD'ing and cutting myself about three weeks after he moved in. Ken's stuck by me throughout all this. He's cared for me and looked after me.

I tried to hang myself, had my breakdown, ended up sectioned and in hospital. That's when all my past caught up with me and come crashing into the back of me. All my shit has come with me. I'm alone here in this world.

When I look in the mirror now, I don't know what I see. I see a trapped androgynous being. I still feel that I am somatically adjusting. I feel like Simone, I feel like a she, but I don't feel I look it when I look in the mirror. I don't know what I see. When I had my breasts done, I had three months to adjust, I'm only just beginning to adjust to them. When I'm out of it, on drugs, I like myself, a beautiful, young girl. When I'm not out of it … I'm very confused at what I see. As a kid, looking in the mirror, I couldn't understand what I was seeing. I'm now twenty-two and I still don't understand what I see. Maybe it's because I'm changing all the time. My emotions have never been settled.

I feel like the ugly duckling; sad, on its own, worthless. I'm building on getting better, getting well. What the duckling wants is somebody to love it, tell her she's nice and lovable, someone to take care of her.

I know that when I was a kid I was lost, but I wasn't conscious of it, only subconscious. Lately I've realized that I suppose all my life I've been lost. It's only recently I've been able to put that in words, 'I'm lost.' It's the first time I've found those words and can say that's how I feel. I guess I'm in touch now. I am lost.

Peter's one of my problems, he's in the back of my mind. I suppose he is my twin, and I love him. I never really sit to think about how I feel about Peter. Probably because it is too painful. Well, there's lots of issues in my life that are too painful. I never talked with him, when I ran away. I never explained why I was leaving him. I feel so guilty about that. We have been in touch and one day, soon, I will explain to him.

114

I find it difficult to trust people. Throughout my whole life people have let me down and when they do let you down, you believe everybody's going to do it. I haven't got friends. I know you don't pick them off trees but I haven't. The only friend I have got, Steve, I'm losing because he's out on smack. We didn't just do drugs together; we were still there for each other. But there's nothing I can do with him. I can't stop him taking smack. You watch someone you care about just going downhill, and there's fuck all you can do about it. He promises me he won't take it, but it's not like that, is it?

I would like a couple of friends. Sometimes I feel it would help to have a transsexual friend on the same lines as me. Because there are things about my sexuality I feel I have to sort out, decide and understand. I've gone off the rails a bit, being a transsexual. Drugs have interrupted it, being with Nigel interrupted it as I didn't take the hormones, because I felt so bad about myself. Now I'm getting older, I must start looking after myself as a transsexual seriously, by taking my hormones regularly.

Lots of transsexuals don't think the way that I think. A lot of pre-ops would deny that they ever used down there, because they think it makes them a man. Believe you me, most transsexuals are the most small-minded and ignorant people: they are like a stereotyped man. I think it's one big male ego. The biggest male ego going; who gets the biggest tits done? When? Who's the prettiest? Who's the best? Who's the one that don't get sussed? Who does get sussed? Who's doing what? That's not how it should be. Just bitches, just like men with cars; go out and get the girls. You must have the operation, if you don't have the operation you are not a transsexual. They are stupid, small-minded. It's not the way it should be at all.

There are a lot of very unhappy transsexuals out there. When they've had their breasts done and downstairs done, they've achieved what they set out to do. Then what do they do? What else is there to do in life? I don't see myself as that. That's where it stops. I could be a transsexual and a social worker, I could be a therapist, I could have goals and aims in life, see the world. Forget what's downstairs. It's not an issue, whether I want to keep down there or not; I am a transsexual. I can never get away from that. Nor can they. That's why I don't get on with them. A lot of transsexuals would be disgusted to hear me say that, eight and a half inches on the phone, but a lot of them do it themselves! They do it, but won't admit. Which I think is wrong.

I know a lot of transsexuals who've had the operation recently. They've had it done for all the wrong reasons. You've got to realize you are vulnerable. I do still know that I will still wake up in the morning and be lost. It's not going to make everything wonderful. You see that's where they think their operation is going to make everything go away. The pain of everything go away. How come when they have had their operation, they are out on the gay scene every weekend, some women they are! They'll tell me I'm less of a woman than they are. But I don't class myself as a woman anyway, I'm transsexual. I'd like to find someone on the same wavelength as me, I think it would help.

Four months after my breakdown, I've got my social worker, my psychiatrist, my GP and Ken. People to help me sort out my life.

I have to work through what I'm working through. I'm not that naive to think that prostitution helps, it's abusive, but the money these fucked-up men bring me, to do what I tell them to do, is so camp! I am a fighter. I have to be to get through what I've been through. I'm a fighter always.

I feel like the ugly duckling in the transition, and I know she's going to spring into a beautiful swan. I always said I wanted a fairy-tale ending.

'Ryan'

I'm twenty-four years old. My parents are West Indian and I was born in north London. I never knew my father. I don't know anything about him, not even his name. I think if I were to meet him, I would be very angry with him. I wouldn't have had to go through half the things I did, if he'd been there. I would very much like to have had a dad, I needed one.

My mother was very young when she had me; sixteen. She didn't get on very well with her mum. Her mum was very strict with her, and used to make her do all the housework. She was picked on to do all the horrible jobs in the house, she felt that she was hated by her mum. She got a lot of stick when she found out she was pregnant with me, and was thrown out of the home.

I was born with club feet. No muscle whatsoever below the knee, just skin and bone. I was straight away admitted to the wards, where I had one operation after another. I was still in plaster when I was taken home six months later. The hospital did more damage than good and they fucked up. I was later transferred to Great Ormond Street hospital where a pin was put in each foot and I was in plaster again. The operations and check-ups carried on for ten years.

When I was at the age where I should have been walking around, I couldn't. I had both legs in plaster and had to be pushed around all the time. I moved around by shuffling my bottom along the floor. Because I couldn't walk or put any weight on my feet, I remember having to climb upstairs by pulling myself up with my arms and dragging the rest of me up behind.

When my plaster was finally taken off, my mum had got to a stage where she had become quite fed up, with always having to drag me around with her everywhere for four years. She had to carry me on and off the buses; up and down to the hospital all the time. The hospital visits took up a whole day: getting there, waiting for my appointment and getting back. After a while she let me know she really resented it.

With my plaster off, I learned to walk for the first time. I was four years old. I was sent to playschool. It was in a big church with stained glass. I tried to look out of the windows and felt really trapped and scared because I couldn't see out. I was crying because I couldn't see out. Later, I got used to it. When I got there, with my new-found freedom with being able to use my legs, I used to run straight for the tricycle and cycled around on it all day long. I couldn't put it down. I didn't mix with the other children.

I wasn't really aware that my legs were any different to anybody else's until I went to school. I suddenly had all these insults thrown at me: 'black cripple', 'crippled wog'. It was the first time I really became aware that my legs were different. It was made worse because I always had to wear shorts as my mother refused to let me wear long trousers. I asked my mother what a 'wog' was. I didn't understand her reply: I didn't understand what racism was.

I was very much a ladies' man in school. I tried to grab every single girl I possibly could. I used to get kisses off the odd few. I think school was a piss really. Maybe a bit of freedom as well. Up until then the only kids I really saw were my cousins.

My mum and I travelled all over London, living in various bedsits and bed and breakfasts. It wasn't until I was about ten that we stayed somewhere long-term. We stayed in places for short periods of time, like every few months. She needed help. She had a social worker for a couple of visits, but she thought social workers were nosy, interfering busybodies, and didn't see anyone again.

I could read and write by the time I left primary school. My mum taught me. I remember at this particular school they used to give us

118

this book. We had to read a certain amount of sentences each week and I'd got really fed up with this stupid book. You know the sort of book, 'Here is Jack, here is Jill', that sort of crap. I got so fed up with it that, one day, my teacher called me up to read my little passage and I just read the whole book. I didn't stop to get my breath, I just read it to get it out of my way. My teacher then realized that I could read, and from then on I was allowed to pick my own books.

When I was seven, I remember some people came to the door. They started chatting to my mum; it was then she became a Jehovah's Witness. She became worse to me. She took a lot of things from the Bible literally. 'Spare the rod, spoil the child.' She took that very seriously. She believed that, if you love your child, you discipline him. She would always tell me the reason she hit me was because she loved me.

I then got knocked around most days. I was terrified. She had a great hold over me. She was a big woman, used her strength and size as a weapon against me. She would literally sit on top of me, on the floor, and beat me so I couldn't move. She usually beat me on my arse, on my legs, and on my hands. Many times I banged my head on the wall while she was hitting me. My legs came up in big bumps. On those days I'd be allowed to wear long trousers to school; otherwise they'd all know she'd beaten the crap out of me.

The beatings didn't get noticed at school, because I was never allowed to do games, because of my bad feet. No one saw the state of me. Before she became a Jehovah's Witness she used to slap me, but then she'd apologize and we'd apologize to each other. But then that stopped, and she became more as if she enjoyed doing it. Gradually each session of beatings would have more hits; more and more lashes. She'd use anything she could lay her hands on: bits of wood, cable. The cable stung like hell. She used small leather belts because they hurt the most. On your hands, that was the worst. She would pull her whole arm back as far as she could, put her whole weight into the lash on my hand. It would sting and I would feel it throbbing and put my hand between my legs. Then she would make me put my hand back and do it again, even though it was really red. Then she would do the other hand. I dared not move my hand because I'd get an extra lash. I had to stand there and let her do it. I couldn't fight back. I did speak to a teacher once, but then it got back to my mum and I was in even more trouble.

We had aunts and uncles who lived in London. I used to see them quite regularly. They always thought that my mum was much too strict on me, so they would have big arguments with her over me. But she felt she was bringing me up in the right way, they were just interfering. She wouldn't listen to anybody else. They knew she went overboard with me; but it was hopeless trying to tell her.

I couldn't do anything. I couldn't move without her say-so. It came to the stage where I was frightened to be around her. There would be some mornings when, if she had been woken up by the neighbours during the night, she would be in a foul mood. I would hide myself in the bedroom. I just knew that if I just did the slightest thing wrong, all that anger would be taken out on me. It got to the stage that sometimes, I did things to please her in order that she wouldn't get annoyed with me over anything. It was through fear that I learned to do this, rather than trying to be kind.

She used to take a lot of her temper out on me. She'd always find reasons to have a go at me. She often told me that she hated the fact that she had to keep taking me to and from the hospital. As I grew up, I began to hate myself for having the disability because she hated it. It became harder for me, as I grew older, to accept it. That's where I have my problem now. The fact that I can't accept it because of the way she treated me; even though it wasn't my fault. I didn't ask for it. I was made to feel I was responsible for it.

Up until I was fourteen, the only other kids that I ever saw out of school were my cousins. I had a lot of cousins; I grew up with them. There were quite often times when they would stay at our house, and we would stay at theirs. I liked them. They were someone for me to play with. When I was at home, I had no one to play with. I can't remember what games we used to play. It's strange, I remember very little about my cousins, even from spending so much time with them.

A lot of our time together was spent studying for the meetings. They were Jehovah's Witnesses, too. We used to go about three times a week. It was very stressful and boring for children: very, very boring.

When I was about nine, I remember me and my boy cousins rolling around on the floor on top of each other without any clothes on. I got quite excited over that, but lots of boys go through that stage.

I used to spend a lot of time on my own, indoors, as a kid. I always had this wanting to be a singer. Every weekend I used to get all my records out, play them and I'd sing along. But, whenever my mother came into the same room, I'd stop singing straight away. To this day, I can't sing in front of, or with other people. I was too scared to show that I was happy, or that I was angry, I was too scared to breathe almost with her about.

I started the violin at primary school. I wasn't very good at reading music but I could play fine. I spent a lot of time listening to music on my own. My taste was influenced by what my mum listened to. She was into classical music and a lot of old stars like Johnny Mathis and Nat King Cole.

When I was ten we moved to a house with a garden. There was a big rubbish tip there and I found things to mess around with. I used to hoard lots of bits and pieces of useless junk. I used to play around with the old cars and pretend I was driving them. I used to ride my bike a lot. In one place where we lived, we used to have two sheds and one of them was mine. I used to spend a lot of time in there, having all sorts of bits and pieces of my own in there. It was a bit like a tree house, but on the ground. It had shelves up; I had loads of things like nuts and bolts, nails and things that were quite useful really. I used to store them all in this shed. I was good at fixing things, electrical things. I used to take things apart a lot. I'd find old TVs and radios and take bits off them and keep the bits and pieces.

When I began my secondary schooling, I got sent to a high school for boys. My mother sent me to this school because she said I was messing around with the girls too much, and not concentrating on my school-work. That wasn't entirely true, I played kiss chase in the playground, and even showed one girl my wanny [personal word for penis – 'my wand'] underneath a table, in a class full of kids; but I never actually even had a girlfriend.

At this school I thought I managed to make friends easily. I soon found out that most of them weren't friends at all. Many took the piss out of me because of my feet.

The Jehovah's Witnesses and my mother had taught me to turn the other cheek, but, when I got to secondary school, racism and my disability was something that upset me very much. Every day I went in, someone would insult me in some way. I was very upset by this constant name calling: 'black cripple', 'monkey', 'nigger' and all this kind of stuff, I really used to hate it and started to hate going to school.

My mum told me not to hang about with the black kids, they were trouble-makers. But the trouble-makers were both black and white. They were those who needed help from the teacher, and what happened was a lot of kids just got fed up of trying to learn, so they just didn't bother and ended up causing trouble. The kids who knew everything were encouraged to keep working hard, and those who were a little bit slower were just kind of left, or put in a lower class. It happened to me. I got put in a lower class for maths. I had real big problems with maths. I really couldn't grasp it. All they did was put me in a pathetic silly little class that really didn't help me learn any more about maths. In the end, I failed my maths exams and just gave up. The two subjects I did well in were science and English. I got a grade two in both of those.

As I got older, from the age of twelve, I found it easier to control white people's insults. I could beat them up if it came to it. I could push them around or whatever. My upper body was well built and developed and I was also good at shouting and screaming at people to keep them away. That way I ensured that they did not give me any hassle. They would respect me: well, not really *respect* me, but fear me. It was easier for me to have that bit of a hold on them, it kind of made me feel better as it stopped some of the insults.

I had to be careful, though, because if any word got back to my mum that I hadn't been behaving, I would have been in severe trouble. But sometimes I got so mad when I was provoked, I was so angry I had to fight back. I couldn't turn the other cheek any longer.

I felt quite cut off from everyone. I so much wanted to be a part of everyone's little group, and I never was. I was always the outsider, always trying to squeeze in. I would hear kids agreeing to meet up later on in the evening. No one ever asked to meet up with me. I always felt quite rejected. It's quite funny, because it's been the same story all through my life; always trying to get into everyone's little group; trying so hard for people to like me; and always being pushed away, or ignored like I don't have feelings, or that I am not worth being someone's friend. It's not surprising I've lacked self-confidence for most of my life.

My feet were a lot better by the time I was twelve, although there was still some pain. I had one more operation to go, which should have been my last. But my mother had had enough of taking me to and from the hospital, and she said wouldn't take me anymore. So I never had the operation.

My mother said you can't keep using your feet as an excuse. You've got to just get on with it. I was never really into sports. So I never really tried my hardest. I hated football, I could never figure out the rules, or which way I was supposed to be running, or what I was supposed to be doing.

When I was fourteen, I was taking a big part in the sermons. On this particular day, I was supposed to go up and give this talk that my mother had put together. I had to read this passage out of the Bible to her first, but I couldn't pronounce a word. She became more and more annoyed with me because I couldn't pronounce this word. So, in the end, she took me into the bathroom, filled up a bowl full of water and stuck my head in it. She'd make me say this word again, and then I'd get it wrong again, and she'd push my head in again, and she'd do it, for what seemed like ages. It scared the hell out of me. For something so petty as mispronouncing a word, she shouldn't have done that to me; she didn't have any remorse. I developed a permanent fear of water. I have a lot of fears and insecurities which are a result of being mistreated.

From the age of fourteen, I knew I was attracted to or turned on by men. I thought it was a stage I was going through. It got serious when I used to kiss some guy at school. I remember bringing him home, and I used to really fancy him. Because we were in my house, I couldn't do anything, not that I had any idea what to do. Everyone used to say he was gay. They all used to taunt him and I joined in with taking the piss out of him as well. Yet I used to fancy him like crazy. I used to fancy quite a lot of the guys at school. I wasn't really around girls much; my cousins were boys, and I went to an all-boys school.

It wasn't until I was sixteen I definitely realized I was gay. I knew then it was no longer a stage I was going through. The Jehovah's Witnesses said that homosexuality was evil, a complete no-no. It wasn't even discussed. It was the lowest of the low you could possibly be. That has been very hard for me to deal with. There was no one around I could talk about it with. I didn't have anyone. No way could I talk to my mum. I was in a lot of turmoil, and so I started to throw myself at women just to prove to myself that I wasn't gay. Every single woman that walked past me was a potential girlfriend. This went on for two years, when I eventually did go out with a girl.

I was always very involved with my faith. At sixteen, I was the youngest person in our congregation to get baptized. However, not long after that, my mum became very disappointed with the Church, she said a lot of people were talking about her behind her back, because she was a single mother and she wasn't happy with that. She never went again.

I stayed on for maybe a couple of months after that, but then I gradually lost interest. I wanted more than what was being offered. There wasn't very much support or anything for me. I no longer felt that I belonged there.

Now I don't wish to have anything to do with religion at all. I've lost all my belief, I even find it difficult to believe there's a god. Up to maybe a year or two years ago, I was still scared about things I had done, feeling very guilty, and thinking I'm going to go straight to hell for being a homosexual for the life I've led. The way I see it now, I may as well enjoy my life. There's no point in living life being totally restricted.

I left school at sixteen. This man came round to our house with my uncle and my aunt. They brought him down for a visit. I didn't pay any attention to him. The next time I saw him, he took my mum for a night out. Then she showed me this letter that he'd sent her. I remember saying to her, 'Why don't you let him stay the night?' She said, 'Oh, you don't mind?' I said, 'No.' I said that because she made me feel that I had made her miss out on everything. In a way, I really did want her to be happy. She was happy when she met this bloke. I didn't want to stand in the way of her. I didn't want her to feel that she didn't have to give him up because of me. So he stayed for the night.

Very shortly after that they were engaged, and, before I knew it, she was pregnant. It all happened very quickly. It was very hard for me to deal with. One minute he was there, and I'd seen him a couple of times: the next minute they were getting married and she was having a baby. The sudden change was too much for me. It was awful to have another man around the house. It made me feel very unwanted, excluded. Until that point, I was man of the house. If furniture needed moving, I would move it. If the shed needed cleaning out, if something needed to be put up, it would be my job. All of a sudden, he could do all that. I wasn't needed. Just the fact that I was useful made me feel wanted. Once that was taken away, I no longer felt wanted. She didn't need me anymore.

I really tried to get on with him. He made it very difficult; so I just gave up. I found I was working so hard to come to terms with this person, whom I hardly knew, and he made it very difficult. He made me feel stupid. When I tried to talk to him, he would always say, 'What are you talking about? You talk so much stupidness.' He would always say that to me, no matter what I'd said to him. In the end, I gave up. I even worked with him for a little while, hoping that we could understand each other more, get to know each other more. It didn't work. It was me who tried to encourage the relationship. But I was being blamed by my mother and him for it not working, although I was trying my best.

My mum made it painfully clear she didn't like me being there. She told me several times she hated me. She often said to me, 'I could have had you adopted, but I didn't. I stayed with you. I looked after you but you've caused me all this trouble.' I really wished I had been adopted and put in a home. I think I would have been far happier. I used to think, whatever happened to my real dad? He should be here to look after me.

I actually wrote my mum a nasty letter which I left lying around for her to find. I wrote, *When you had sex you got pregnant, how can you take all this out on me? It's your fault, you've got to deal with it. You can't take it out on me: it's not my fault. I didn't ask for all this to happen.*

She was looking for an excuse to get me out of the house. So when I stayed out too late at a party she kicked me out. She wouldn't let me in the house that night. I had to spend the night sleeping in my shed, soaked to the skin because I got wet coming home. In the morning I knocked on the door, and she told me to pack my stuff and get out.

I did not know the first thing to do. I did not know how to find somewhere to live. I was sixteen. I had no idea. I didn't know about signing on, but she did give me one word of advice – go to the social security office. I went there and signed on. They gave me the address of some hostel or other.

Getting in touch with my relatives was always arranged through my mum. She'd ring them up and sort out when we'd go round there, or they'd come round here; I never contacted them. So I didn't even know how to get in touch with them. I was brought up very sheltered and unable to look after myself. Getting thrown out was very scary for me. I was very depressed; suicidal. Yes, suicidal. I tried twice to do myself in. I didn't really want to do it; I just wanted someone, more than anything else, to say and show me that they cared.

At that time I just felt like everyone else was going out, partying and having a good time; and there was I, trying to find somewhere to live. I really felt that I lost a lot of my childhood then because I had to grow up. I couldn't be carefree and go out every weekend, go partying or whatever. I had to find a job, pay my rent, buy food, it was a very hard time. I was really lonely as well. I had no one with me. I don't know how I got through it all.

When I left home I was so unprepared to face the world; it was like a big shock for me. I was so naive about people. People stepped all over me right, left and centre; people hurt me, and I didn't know any better. I just let them do it. All I knew was family. It was real shit, what she did.

I had to just get on with it. I knew there was no one there to go to or anyone to talk to, help me or advise me. So I just had to do it by myself. I found some strength. I moved around a hell of a lot. Things happened; I had to leave places. Most of them were either hostels or rooms in houses. I ended up sleeping rough for many periods. I slept around Camden on park benches. I couldn't find anywhere where I could settle down. There was always some problem with either the people I was sharing with, or the landlady; there was always *something*. It was a horrible time. I had so many bad experiences in houses that I stayed in.

I moved into one place. I found out about it through an agency. I knew something was not right. I felt tense as soon as I met the landlady. Yet I moved in because I was desperate. Then one night, shortly after, I got attacked by her. She was an alcoholic, and it completely scared the crap out of me. She burst into my room in the middle of the night, she tried to throw my stereo out the window, and she started kicking and screaming at me saying I'd killed her baby. She was absolutely crazy: it was a nightmare. I ended up ringing the police because I didn't know what to do. She went absolutely livid. Then the police came; she went down the stairs screaming rape and they ran up and saw me standing there bawling my eyes out. They said, we should take you away, you don't want to stay here, so I had to leave the place.

I was a mess, a complete mess. I was in tears, it really frightened me. I phoned my mother up in the middle of the night, she said to me come back home. That's the first time we'd spoken since she'd thrown me out, a year before.

She was OK at first. Then she started acting really funny towards me and she kept saying things like, she knew what I was capable of, that she didn't trust me and didn't know what I was going to do next. I couldn't understand why she kept saying these things. I had given her no reason to suggest that I was going to do anything to her, but she seemed to have some idea in her head that I was.

I tried to be friends with her, tried to please her, tried to make life easier for her; but she just took advantage of it. That hurt me. We'd go shopping and she'd be putting all these things in the basket, and then we'd get to the till, and she'd say, I've got no money. I'd regularly end up paying £40 for her. I was buying the kids' clothes, I was taking them for days out; I didn't mind, they were my two new brothers, and I got really close to them. It was just the fact that she just abused me that way. If I came to the front door, and I didn't have a bottle of alcohol in my hand for her, she wouldn't open the door to me. She drank a lot, she could put it away. She always has done, she used to get angry if anyone even so much as suggested that she had a problem.

Her husband was still there, but she wanted him out the house. She'd had the kids and she didn't need him anymore. She used to do vile things to him as well. At that time, it was funny to me, because I didn't like him very much. I didn't have anything to do with him and I was either out working or out with my brothers. When I think back on it, I think she was really evil.

He didn't do anything, he didn't take an interest in their kids, he never spent money on them, never took them out. I felt bad because they were my brothers and I loved them. It was still part of his duty to look after them, care for them, and give them what they needed. At least I was able to look after them for the couple of months that I was to stay at home.

She got pregnant again, so I had to leave. There wasn't enough room. I wanted to be part of my brothers' lives; although they were young, I was very close to them. They always looked forward to me coming home from work.

Just coming up to eighteen and I found myself on my own again. I met a girl, Kathy. She was white and had just had a baby by an African guy. She was living in a half-way house for single mothers and their babies. I hadn't had sex with anyone before. She was my first. We were together for about a year.

128

She was completely hopeless at looking after her baby. I was better at looking after the child than she was. She went shopping and she'd forget to buy nappies or food. How can you do that if you've got a baby? She was so hopeless that a social worker threatened to take the baby away. I went to see the social worker and sorted things out, saying I'd take responsibility for both of them and their debts. I more or less looked after that baby. I wasn't dumped on, I took it on myself to look after that child. When I was working or signing on, I had no money for myself, it went on her and the kid. Exactly the same as when I was living at home.

There was talk of us getting engaged and then the turning-point came. We had a row because I found out she was sleeping with every Tom, Dick and Harry. Two doors down from where she lived there was another couple and they had a relative staying with them, a Scottish blond guy. We met him a couple of times. Me and him ended up getting off with each other and that was it. We got chatting; I told him I was really fed up with women. There were communal showers at their place. He asked me if I'd go in there with him. He didn't need to ask me twice. The next thing I knew, he asked me if I wanted to give him a blow job. Of course, I willingly accepted and that was it. I just got on with it. My first time I had sex with a guy. I quite liked him, but nothing happened again after that. He said for us to meet there next day, and that it would be my turn next. He never turned up. I felt really guilty afterwards, and told Kathy. Things deteriorated for us from then on and we split up.

Still eighteen, I started working for a club. I used to work three nights a week glass-collecting. After I'd been there a few weeks, I was getting very good at glass-collecting. Then they asked me if I wanted to do some work during the day. There was a maintenance guy there and he needed some help. I said yes. So I started working for a few hours during the day there as well. Then eventually they made me head glass-collector. I was in charge of five or six glass-collectors. This meant telling them what bars they were going to be working on, and what breaks they were going to get. Generally kicking them up the arse if they weren't doing enough work. That was pretty good, I've never had that sort of power or authority before.

I was a horrible person to work for. I really did work those people to the bone. I wouldn't let them skive off at all. A lot of them really hated me for it: then a lot of them respected me, because they knew that I got the job done at the end of the day. They knew that although I was hard on them, that if they worked and I was happy with their work, I'd be good to them. I'd tell them that they'd done a good job at the end of the night. I also got a number of people fired for not working properly. A couple thought it would be good to skive off and chat up the girls, they ignored my warnings to get on with their work, and got fired.

Then I was asked if I wanted to do all the cellar work. I said yes. I got shown how to do that in just ten minutes. He just went, 'You do this, you do that', and then, 'Right, I'm off; 'bye!' I thought, Oh my god. I've never touched a beer barrel in all my life. But I picked things up, and got to be very good at sorting out the cellars. I was taking in deliveries and ordering, doing all the paperwork, everything. I really got into that. Then they made me head cellarman.

I was doing the cellars and maintenance work during the day, and doing the glass-collecting by night. I then decided I didn't want to do the glass-collecting any more. I'd got tired of it. I really wanted, for ages, to do the lighting. Then the guy who did them decided he didn't want to come in one night. He asked me to do the lights for him. There was a big to-do. The manager didn't want me to leave the glass-collecting and do the lighting, and so I left. He offered me more money and let me start doing the lighting which is what I really wanted to do. I got to work my way up to do the decent jobs, because I'm very inquisitive. I have to ask lots of questions and I watch a lot. That place was a big part of my life. I was there practically twenty-four hours a day. Very often I would sleep there after doing the cellar work. I'd work during the day, have a few hours' sleep at the club, then I'd go upstairs and get dressed for the night shift.

I really enjoyed the lighting, really loved it. When I started, I didn't know very much about it, but I was very good at it. This guy said to me that I'd got the right rhythm. I didn't know very much about how to use the whole system, only one or two bits, but I more or less taught myself how to use the whole system. Every week I would find out something new or find something different or some different effect that I could produce. Gradually, I learnt how to use the whole thing myself. I got well known for my light shows and lots of people came down to see them; the head directors – even the CID! They all used to always ask me for a light show. Working there was one of the things I'm proudest of in my life. I'd worked my way up from such a small little job and got where I wanted. I worked hard and stuck with it.

When I first started working there it was like one big family; everybody got on with everyone, everyone had a good laugh, everyone enjoyed themselves. It was a very happy time of my life. I also came out to everyone there, everybody accepted me.

I worked there for three years. I spent two of those years not ever meeting a partner, it was very lonely for me even though I was happy at work. I often dreamed of meeting someone and being in love.

It was in my third year there, aged twenty, I met my first boyfriend; he was at the once-a-week gay night at the same club I worked in. I gave him my phone number and to my surprise he rang me. We met up and had two whole days of unadulterated sex. Then some bitch opened her big mouth to him, and told him I was crazy about him. I went round to see him and he told me he didn't want to see me again. I was devastated and cried my eyes out. I don't think I'll ever get over him; he was the first guy I had properly slept with and I fell in love with him.

I'd seen my mum a few times after I was kicked out of home. She had been round to my place once and I'd been round to the home; really to see my two brothers and my new sister.

This time, I went home with a female friend from work, to tell my mum that I was gay. I was tired of fighting this battle inside of me that what I was doing was wrong, and I shouldn't be doing it. I didn't want to hide it any more. It had cut me up so much, for so long. It had taken me so long to come out, and so long to come to terms with it. I knew she would find out sooner or later. I'd finally got round to sleeping with a guy; I knew the time was right for her to know. I could no longer hide it from her, or myself anymore. I came out with a bang; it was like – I'm really here now. It was such a big relief for me when I came out; god, like a massive weight had been lifted off me.

I told her I was gay, and she said, 'What do you mean you are gay?' I said, 'I'm gay.' She said, 'You are just being silly, you are just saying that because you've split up with Kathy.' I said, 'No I'm not; I've met someone.' She said to me, 'Have you slept with him?' I said yes. She went quiet, and said, 'Fine; don't ever come here again. I don't want to see you, or hear from you ever again. You are not to see the children ever again.' I just broke down and cried. At the time in a way, I was glad because I felt that she had used me for so long and I felt that I was better off not being with her, but after a while I began to miss it all; seeing her, seeing my brothers, but by then it was too late.

I didn't want to go through my life not telling her. In a way I'm glad I told her, but in another way I didn't like having to give my family up; although I never really felt much a part of it. I was someone who just provided the cash to keep it going. I thought she would appreciate the fact that I was honest with her; but she just didn't want to know.

I think it's probable that I'm gay because I felt emotionally that women couldn't provide me with what I wanted. I think I've probably been put off by women, because of my mother, and also other girls that I have met. For a long while I was very scared of black women, because they can be very overbearing, and tough as well. I mean who knows; if I had been brought up differently I may have turned out straight. When I was younger, I found women attractive, but sexually men were more attractive to me. The fact that most of my school life was spent in all-boys schools may also have had an influence on me.

When I first came out I wore outrageous clothing, lots of make-up, but that didn't suit me too well. I looked at myself, and just thought, this isn't really me. I was attracting the wrong people as well, so I stopped it. I skipped between camp and butch. I can be outrageously camp one day and the next I could pass for a straight guy. I prefer not to stick to being one thing the whole time. I enjoy exploring both sides of my character. I have been butch in bed with men, and a few times I have gone the other way. Everyone has a feminine side. A lot of people are too scared or don't wish to explore it or show it. It's as if they feel they will be less of a man for it. A few people have tried to make me be this big bad-arse black man, which I am certainly not. I have a tough side to me, but I rarely show it, and those who have witnessed it did not enjoy it too much. My camp side tends to come out when I'm enjoying myself or when I am in the company of other queens. My other side, being just straight-like, is my more serious side, which is usually for when I'm feeling like a deep conversation or everyday circumstances. I'm quite happy with the way I am.

I know most black straight people have got a really bad attitude towards gay people, especially black gays, more so than white gays. A lot of white people accept it, or put up with it, although they don't agree with it. As long as they don't have to see it and are not approached by anyone gay. The majority of black straight people won't accept it. I've seen interviews on TV and their whole attitude towards it is just very scary. I think that's why a lot of black gay guys are so outrageously camp. As a whole, black men are scared of femininity in men because a lot of them have this very big macho image of themselves. Femininity scares them more than the actual person being gay. That's why so many black gay men are so effeminate; it's like they are revolting against the whole big tough macho image that most black men have.

I've spent a long time looking for someone who would give me everything that I didn't have. I spent my whole life craving for love. I go to any lengths I can to get it, which has caused me so many problems. I've slept with people I basically don't want to be with, I didn't fancy them, wasn't attracted to them physically. I stayed with them. I'd go to any lengths to have people with me, to be around me. I think it stems back to when I was back at home and I always wanted to be hugged and have affection but never got it. I was never emotionally fulfilled.

I was twenty-one when the club got closed down. I went through a severe depression, I even attempted suicide. One night I was really fucked off. I decided to go to Busby's and get drunk. I met a guy there called Ray. He was really horny. I got talking to him, and then I got off with him. He was nineteen, with blonde hair, a beautiful face and body to match. I was disappointed when I found out he was a rent boy. I hoped at the time that I could persuade him to give it up. He spent a few nights with me and it felt so good to have someone with me. He was so perfect. I'd waited so long for the right person and then I couldn't satisfy him sexually. I felt such a failure.

I was due to meet him a few days later and he stood me up. I think I must have scared him away because I told him I loved him. He left his track suit at my place. Every time I saw it, I cried. He stole my pair of nearly new trainers. I couldn't understand why he left me, I hoped he would come back.

I met him about a month later, back in Busby's. He told me he had been arrested the day he left my place, and had been inside ever since. He'd just been let out. I was so glad to see him. I couldn't stop hugging and kissing him, I wanted him back so badly. He said he had to go and talk to someone. I never saw him again. I thought about him for ages after that.

I fucked up so many relationships. I realized how badly I'd been affected emotionally, I found I was jealous, vicious and moody. I found myself treating people the way my mum treated me, yelling at them, bullying them and being spiteful when I knew they wouldn't retaliate. That scared me.

There were times when I wished really evil things would happen to her. Sometimes I really wished that she could be lying somewhere in pain so she could realize how much pain I'd been through. I wouldn't have pissed on her if she was burning, I really wouldn't.

Still twenty-one years old, I got a job at Burger King. I learnt how to run every single station. I could work on the Whopper bar, I could work on the Burger bar, I could work on the speciality, I could do the front counter, I could do the lot.

The constant standing up at work made my feet painful and stiff. By this time they were full of arthritis. I found it difficult getting upstairs and to move around.

I was working eight-hour shifts every day with just a half-hour break. I spent two hours walking from home to work and work to home, to save money on my fares; it was too much. I became very irritable. I didn't get on with anyone, because I used to be shouting at everyone, it wasn't working out.

The wages were so crap that I couldn't live off them. I was getting paid £80 a week to live on and my rent was £50 a week. It was ridiculous trying to live on that amount of money. My fares to get to work would have been £10 per week if I hadn't walked. I just couldn't support myself, and I was borrowing money which I hadn't a hope of repaying. One day I'd had enough, and walked out of my job.

I couldn't get any dole money. If you leave your job without proper reason they don't give you any money. I didn't really think of using my feet as an excuse to say this is why I left my work. I had to wait for the normal time before I could get dole. It was something stupid like twenty-five weeks.

When I worked at the Burger King in Victoria, I used to use the cottage there. I bumped into these two white guys and started hanging around with them. I really fancied one of them. They did the rent. One of them suggested that I do it, because of my money problems. At the time, I didn't really want to do it at all. It didn't really strike me as something that I could do, but I desperately needed the money to live. The guys said, you'd make a fortune out there, there's not many black guys who do it. So I decided to do it.

I was twenty-two when I went on the rent. I was out every night around Earls Court and the Dilly until five in the morning. It started off as a kind of adventure. I was out late every night. There were loads of people around and I was having a good laugh with everyone; it was a sense of community. Earlier on in the evening, it was good fun and really exciting; out with everyone. Then, later on, the boys started to get serious and to earn their money. They all seemed to have their friend who they used to hang around with. They were all white. It seemed to be a race thing. They didn't want to have me around them. I was an outsider. It would scare off business or whatever. It was a case of they'd stick with each other, so I usually ended up on my own.

I knew from the first time that I did it, I wasn't going to get anywhere with it. I hated it. It was a nightmare for me every time someone picked me up. Although I needed the money, weeks went by when I didn't do a punter and didn't have a penny to my name. It was literally a case of sleeping wherever, and getting food wherever I could; out the bins, backs of restaurants, wherever. I went really down at that point. I was very low, yet my pride stopped me begging on the streets for money. I couldn't do that. I did in total maybe five different punters over two to three months. I hated every single one of them.

When I was with a punter I had a problem in being in control, taking charge, I couldn't talk to them. They always were in control. I think what made it worse was I felt so vulnerable and used. I should have just dictated what I was going to do or what was on offer, and not let them get away with anything else. I shouldn't have let them do anything I didn't want them to do. I think that's what made it worse, I just felt so dirty the whole time.

Punters want black boys to be slaves. They want to whip and beat them up, and make them wear slave collars. They want to totally degrade the boys. They think all black guys have got big cocks. That's why black guys are supposed to be so popular. My one experience of this was frightening. I went into this room full of straps and other equipment. He really punished me. What scared me most was that I didn't know what he was going to do next. It was one experience I never wish to encounter again.

I always waited for the punters to proposition me. I wasn't able to appear even interested in them. When I went with someone it would be a case of: I'd go there, and get it all over and done with as soon as I could, and I'd be out. If they asked me to stay for a drink or a smoke I didn't. I didn't want to talk to them, or know anything about them. I just wanted to do whatever I had to do, and get it over and done with. I just hated it. I was nervous. I was on edge constantly. They could see I wasn't relaxed, I wasn't happy about things.

The punters I went with were old, white, married businessmen. They used to think that I enjoyed being with them. They wanted to make love, instead of just having sex. They picked me up either on the Dilly or in Earls Court on a street at the back of the Coleherne pub. They all had cars and took me back to their office places. One would play with my balls. I hated it. Then he would want me to lick his balls and for me to suck him off. I saw him again and he wanted me to lick his arse. I refused and so he only paid me half my money – £20. I didn't know how to deal with that. Other guys would have wrecked his place. He kicked me out, and made me find my way back from north London. I never did another punter after that. No one wanted any fucking, thank god – I wouldn't have been able to manage it.

It used to upset me to see the other boys every day, being off their heads and saying they'd just spent £150 on loads of drugs. There was me with nothing to my name, not being able to get myself a meal. I also found it upsetting that they could charge double the amount I did, and would get it. The punters didn't even want to pay the small amount I asked them for. That did not make me feel good. Generally I didn't ask for anything less than £40. That wasn't very much. I knew that I couldn't ask for £80. It was hard when the boys would say they've just done an £80 punter or they'd just made £150.

I made the decision that once I got my dole money I'd give it up; all I really wanted was some money so that I could live. I wasn't successful at renting; I didn't enjoy it; I didn't really see the point in going on with it. I was very lonely, and I hated myself even more. After I stopped doing it, I felt so ashamed and dirty.

Normally, I was very strict about safer sex. It always happened with punters. But there came a point when I was on the rent that I felt so low, that I didn't care whether I got HIV or not. I went with a few guys because I needed love and affection so much; by not using condoms, it made me feel closer to them. I already had it in my mind that I must already have HIV. I went for a test.

Surprisingly it came back negative. After that, I used condoms again for a while. More recently, I started a relationship using condoms, and then my need for affection gets so strong, we stop using them. It never gets discussed until afterwards, and by then it's too late and so we carry on without. I know it's wrong, but I find it very difficult to do otherwise.

One good thing that did come out of doing the rent was that it got me in touch with some services that could help me. Some of the boys told me about Streetwise and I got help in getting specialist accommodation. Their local doctor gave me a sick note so I no longer had to sign on. She referred me to a specialist for my feet. I was officially registered disabled. I had somewhere to hang out in the day and free food to eat. I had counselling and joined some groups which helped build my confidence. I learned to express myself in doing lots of writing and I set about getting my life story together. I learned to use the computer. It was through black workers there that I began to understand my experiences of racism, and learned to relate to and trust in other black people. I found a trust that I have never experienced with white people.

After Streetwise closed down I found myself on my own again. I had the operation on my foot (the one I should have had when I was twelve), and found myself completely housebound. I was in my new home, which I got on the grounds of my long-term disability, without phone, virtually no furniture, and no outside contact and no support. A social worker came round but was really most unhelpful. He built up my hopes, saying he could do this and do that. He promised a phone. He disappeared and did nothing. I tried to ring when I managed to get out of my home, and I was told to ring back later. He knew that I had been on crutches for six months and likely to be for many months to come.

I have been very depressed because the consultant ruined that operation. I was practically housebound for nine months. I had a lot of time to think. I thought about suicide, but couldn't go through with it. I wanted to go to college but couldn't get there. I couldn't understand where all this was going to end.

Music helped me. It is how I've always escaped and relaxed. Depending on what mood I'm in, I'll listen to a certain type of music.

It'll move me on to another level of how I'm feeling in myself. I have to have it, because I find I get very irritable if I don't have music. I've found my moods have been terrible, like someone who's given up smoking, I get very irritable or very ratty. I need music to calm me down or bring me up.

I went out to clubs when I could; I like music with a fast pace. It kept me going, kept me dancing, when the beat went bum, bum, bum, right through my head. I kept on the dance floor, and I didn't have time to think that my feet were hurting me. Even when I was tired, I'd think I've got to dance, and I got high on it.

I constantly daydreamed because I found it difficult to handle reality. I remembered the pleasures of being stoned. I first got stoned when I left home and was in a hostel in Croydon. I just loved it. I could be happy and listen to my music and dance around the bedroom. I could feel comfortable in a group of people and laugh. I could forget about the fact that I was on my own, or that I didn't like where I was living, or that I was having problems; I could just forget it all.

This time round, getting stoned didn't work like that. It made me worse, paranoid, and even more depressed. There was no getting away from my problems now.

I took an ecstasy last Christmas. I was scared about taking it. I took it out of curiosity and because everyone else was doing it. I only took a half. I loved it, I just glowed inside, I was so happy. It was nice; people touching me and holding me. I felt close to everybody. At the end I got paranoid; I heard my mother's voice in the background, 'Next thing you'll be taking drugs!' I've never taken it since. I'm more of an alcohol man and I don't do that very much.

I've had some big turning-points and made some big changes in the last few months. I went down to the Brief Encounter pub and a guy called Jack came over and chatted to me. We met up a couple of times for a drink. He wanted to sleep with me when he first met me, but I thought no; I needed friends, not sexual partners. We've become very good friends. He opened up a new world for me. We always listen to each other's moans. I got so fed up with hearing myself talking about how sorry I was for myself, complaining, and how bitter and twisted I'd become; I realized I had to do something about it, because it wasn't getting me anywhere.

Jack said a lot of things to me that made sense. When I first met him he was into going to straight bars, or mixed places, he was into different things. I found when I went into these bars, I didn't have to worry what I looked like, and what people are thinking about me. I found I could relax and be myself. Unlike how I felt when I had got stuck into the clubs and pubs of the gay scene; people only interested in your looks, it was so bitchy. Now we go bowling, to the pictures, to the theatre together. Having a real friend has helped me see things differently.

I decided I had to put the past behind me and to start living for the future. I spent a lot of time thinking about my family, but thinking about it in a new way. I wanted to see my brothers and sister and my mother. I wrote the following poem:

Mother
For so long I've held a grudge.
How I hated you, how I despised
you. But I was a fool, for me and you
are one; alike thro' and thro'
If I wish to be strong, I must move on.
What you did was wrong.
But I forgive you mum. For what you did
not know, what you did was wrong.
All the bitterness and pain
you passed my way, has now gone.
If I wish to grow; I must defeat
all that was once wrong. I must
go on. I can no longer hate.
The past is gone. The future is where I belong.
For this, I need to be strong.
So now I will move on. Confident that all I suffered,
I will overcome. I understand why you did wrong.

How hard it was to bear child with no father there.
With no one to share your heartbreak and tears.
Now I must find you, and put
right what was wrong. I need you here, mother dear,
for without you, life is bare. I know you cared.
I know your fears and how long they've been there,
for I have also been there: alone, scared
and no one to show they care.
But now the future is here, and I
look for you my dear, for we are
mother and son; your first born.
Help me mother; we need to be strong,
we both need care. So let's forget our tears, and come together
For our lives are bare without each other.

I went round to the house where we lived, to try and see her. The building had been knocked down. That was a real disappointment. I want to sort out something, even if it's to be told to go away. I'm now going to try and find her through the Salvation Army, I've got the phone number.

I've been sorting out my flat, making little things for it, buying little bits and pieces to make it more homely and I've redecorated a lot of it.

I've been getting fit; I've bought a multi-gym through my catalogue and so I've been feeling a lot better about my appearance, building up my body so it will look gorgeous.

I had a lot of anxiety following the operation that went wrong. When I saw the consultant recently, he said the only thing that he could do was to operate to fuse my whole ankle together. I'd have no movement with my ankle. It would be more difficult to move about, but most of the pain would go. He left it with me to decide what I would do. I've decided not to go through with it and waste any more of my life: not doing anything, being housebound again, feeling miserable. I decided it was time to get up and do something. At least I'm mobile now. I need to keep moving to stop the arthritis from seizing my feet up. I no longer have time to moan and think about the pain any more.

Me and Jack discussed going to college. I've now been there a term, doing a two-year course which includes lighting engineering. I'm really enjoying it. I have a reason to get up out of bed every morning. I'm happier now, more of a person, and doing something with my life. I'm a lot more confident. The pain is still there, but I don't have the time to think about it so much now. I'm moving forward. I have a lot of hopes for the future. It's really exciting, thinking about it.

'Adam'

My mum and dad met in the army in Germany, they're both British. He was a lance corporal and she was a major. I was born over there twenty-four years ago. I have an older brother and sister. Seven years after me, came my younger half-brother and then my half-sister.

I didn't get on with my older brother, there was too much of an age gap. As we got older, he was always in trouble. My older sister, Debbie, and I used to get on. She was two years older, we looked like each other and did everything together. She would stand up for me in front of everyone and tell people to leave me alone. For seven years I was the baby of the family. I was a spoilt brat. I was a mummy's boy. I lived for my mum, warped as it may sound. My mum was a friend, she was there for me, and gave me lots of praise. I was a loner as a child and always thought I was different.

My earliest memory goes back to when I was about two. My mum was wearing a wig. She was in the park with her mates and a big gust of wind blew it off. It was really funny to see a woman, six foot one, built like a tank, running around the park with all her mates and all the kids chasing after this wig.

I was taught to speak German as a baby. My mum worked in the weapon stores with a lot of German people, all her friends were German. She did not get on with most of the English people. She didn't like them. My mum and dad spoke German all the time, even at home.

I didn't really know my real dad. He hardly ever came home. He was a bastard. He tried to hit my mum once, she took the frying-pan

143

and hit him one. He never hit her after that. My mum divorced him when I was six. My brother, sister and I were given the choice of who we wanted to live with. My sister Debbie said, 'We don't want our dad,' and so I thought that must be it; I didn't want him. My mum brought me and Debbie back to near Blackpool to live. My brother went to live with our dad.

I went to nursery school in Germany when I was four, and then on to infant school. Because I was so spoilt, I used to think everyone should be doing what I wanted them to do. I thought that I should get all the stars, I should be milk monitor, I should be class monitor. I told the teacher off about the way she spoke to me. I said I'd tell my mum and that she would beat her up. I was always being put in the corner for kicking the desk, and saying you smell of poo-poo, and things like that.

Debbie was in the same school as me in England. She used to get me into trouble. She would tell me to say, 'You are a bitch' and 'Fuck off' to the teachers. I used to do it because she told me to.

At school, I was as thick as two short planks. I used to think I was thick because the teacher said I was. So I used to sit at the back of the class and just muck about. I had to learn to speak English. I was never able to express what I wanted to say. Up until I was eleven, I used to speak very fast with a heavy German accent and people found it difficult to understand me. My mum could see that I was bright but it didn't come out at school. Two years ago, I found out I was dyslexic.

The first time I met my new stepdad was on my seventh birthday. I ran into my mum's bedroom and there he was. Seeing him there was the worst thing that ever happened to me. I was jealous. I hated him. From that point on, our family fell apart, and I lost my closeness to my mum.

I was eight when my mum married him. She was pregnant and later had a baby boy. I became aggressive and used to do things deliberately to annoy people. I used to put the music on really loud in my room and put chairs against the door, so no one could come in. I'd kick things around in the bedroom to make a lot of noise. I'd knock over the TV so no one could watch it. I used to throw my dinner across the room, saying I didn't like it, even if I did. I hated being in my family.

My stepdad had a really good job working in a factory until, one day, he and a colleague were working under a crane. It fell, crushing his leg and crushing his workmate to death. My stepdad had to have his leg amputated.

He was in hospital for ages. I didn't like visiting him, so I didn't go very often. When he came home, he felt so sorry for himself. He wasn't violent at first, he just constantly shouted and drank heavily. He'd drink with the money put by for the rent, electric, etc. and so we were always in debt. But my mum always kept things ticking over so no one knew how bad things really were. Me and my sister hated him so much, we set fire to his bed by putting a lighted candle underneath it.

One day, there was a fire at my home. It was gutted. We had to move. By some great coincidence we moved into a house next door to his weird family. What a mistake.

From the day we moved, he became violent and used to beat my mum. I used to hear her screaming in the middle of the night. One night, me and Debbie went running into their room, because of my mum's yells. He had pinned her to the bed and was trying to strangle her. I was about nine years old, and tall for my age. I jumped on him. He threw me off and started slapping and kicking me. My mum pushed him to the floor, grabbed me and Debbie, and came to sleep in our room.

My stepdad's family was made up of criminals and totally dysfunctional people. One of them was made up of burglars, thieves, arsonist head-cases, abused children, hoax callers, liars and one 'asylum reject' who was my worst nightmare. He used to break into my house and steal things. One time, he burgled my home and stole everything to do with Easter. We had nothing that Easter. My stepdad's family had a lovely Easter on our chocolate. Whenever he broke in, my stepdad always persuaded my mum not to phone the police.

My mum would go shopping for all his family. She'd go to court with whichever one of his twelve brothers or sisters were arrested in the week, and speak on their behalf. She would pay their fines with money she never had.

I found my stepdad's family very confusing. The people I thought were brothers and sisters weren't actually brothers and sisters. They were parents and children involved with each other; brothers and brothers, sisters and sisters, they were all doing it with each other.

There was lots of other stuff that went on. They were burgling everybody's houses. They'd ask me if I wanted to go on a family outing with them, while my mum was out working. I went with them a few times. They used to go into town shoplifting and flogging the goods around the streets. That's the sort of things we did when we went out with the family. That's what normal life was. They told me to take a few things, but the only thing I stole was a wee Wombles man from the market. Later, my mum dragged me back to the stall to take it back.

I didn't like that family. They were dirty. I didn't like them in my house because they smelt. They used to always come to our house, and say can we have this and that. It was never *would you like* this or that. My mum was a very giving person, she never asked for anything, she just constantly gave.

My older brother left our real dad and came to stay with us. He was always getting nicked for assault, burglaries and car thefts. He was in and out of child care places and ended up in borstal.

When I was ten, and off school sick, I asked my sister if she'd stay at home with me. I knew that my worst nightmare the 'asylum reject' knew that I was off school ill, and that he was going to break in again. We waited for him to break into the house and then we both got him. I hit him with a rolling-pin and my sister picked up the scissors and stabbed him in the leg before he ran off. He was twenty-two years old and extremely big built.

The reason I knew he was going to break in was because he had actually broken in before, when he knew I was on my own. He had sexually and physically attacked me. It's too much for me to talk about, even now. On the day that happened, my mum saw me badly bruised. She asked me what had happened. I said I had fallen down the stairs.

My mum had already been to court with this nightmare because he'd attacked another young boy in the same way. She'd lied on his behalf and said he couldn't have done it because he was with her. My mum was very clever in court with the chat, she was very clever and intelligent. This is why she always felt sorry for my stepdad's family and helped them out constantly.

I knew I couldn't trust her: she had let him break into our house loads of times and never phoned the police. She'd protected him over the other boy who'd got attacked.

The only people I've told about my attack was my big brother, who I told six years later. He just reacted with 'I'll kill him', but nothing came of it. After that, I never told anyone again until I was twenty-three, when I told my present partner.

I didn't tell anyone about what went on because what goes on in the house is private. You don't tell other people. I was brought up very much that if you have a slanging match, fine, go out on the streets and have a slanging match. My mum was a right old fishwife, my nanna was a fishwife. But things that go on in the house, that go on behind closed curtains, you don't take them to school and tell the teacher.

Neither do you tell social workers. You don't tell anybody anything. We were always brought up; you never grass on your own. You deal with it yourself. Go round and set fire to their place or something. That's the way we were brought up. We were brought up very moralistic.

My nanna and my mum were brought up with Victorian attitudes. None of us ever talked about things like that. You don't discuss things like that. If things don't seem right, you just ignore it. That's a part of life.

Between the ages of ten and eleven, I went to drama school in the evening. I used to love drama. When I got into a character, everyone would look at me as that character, not who I am. I always strived for perfection in that character and I could really be that person. I was a very shy person normally. Once I played the doctor in *Ring a Ring o' Roses*. That was really brilliant. I can be a very dramatic person. Even now in school, when I come into my job, I'm very dramatic. People say to me, you should be an actor.

When I was eleven, we moved into a caravan by the coast. We had to move away from our home because of all the debts my stepdad and his family had run up. My older sister went to stay with my nanna.

My sister was very much my guardian for years when I was growing up. Her nickname was 'Sledgehammer'. She was always scrapping with someone, and she could head-butt with the best of them. I learned the following Christmas why she was so very aggressive, and why she really went to stay with my nan. It was because she had been raped and abused by my stepfather for years. It came out when she spoke to my nanna just before we moved. That's why she went to live with her.

That Christmas, my mum was very ill. She had been taken into hospital and we were all staying at my nanna's. We were going home Boxing Day. My stepdad had persuaded my nan to allow Debbie to come to the house to help look after us. There was by this time, me, my younger brother aged four and younger sister aged two.

Where I came from, women looked after the home. Men worked. Even though he didn't work, it was accepted that he didn't look after the home. Debbie protested all the way back home. We got back to the house and my stepdad started drinking while we watched TV. Suddenly, he asked me to go to the shop, so I went. Debbie had fallen asleep. It took me a long time to find a shop that was open.

When I got back, Debbie ran to me and dragged me upstairs with my stepdad on our heels. She told me that while I was gone, he had raped her. We ran into the bedroom, locked the door, put the wardrobe and bed against it and stayed there for two days. Every two hours or so, my stepdad would start kicking the door with his false leg and shouting for us to come out. During those two days, Debbie told me about all the things he had done to her. I was even more scared of him after that. We saw him go to the pub. We got dressed for outside, and ran to the phone box and rang my nan to ask if we could go there till my mum came home. I stayed there for two months until my mum came out of hospital.

At school, I didn't like football or cricket. I loved rugby. You got dirty and you could really get it out of your system; get really aggressive and angry. You could run round the pitch and take it out on the ball and run into people. I used to love getting in the rugby scrum, running around the pitch being part of the action.

When I was twelve, we moved again, because of the debts caused by my stepdad. This time, we went to a totally different area about two hours' drive away. I didn't like my new school. I used to get picked on because my stepdad was an arsehole, and everyone gossiped and stuff. I didn't know anyone. The kids picked on me and I never used to fight back. I hated making new friends. It was difficult. I used to sit there quietly, no one talked to me. I would just play around or just sit in the classroom on my own. I'd be physically there, but not mentally.

When I was twelve, my typical day was to take my younger half-brother to school at eight o'clock. Go to school myself. Leave at dinner time. Go down to the fairground. Relieve the people so they could take their breaks and go back to school. I'd leave again at three o'clock. Pick my little brother up from school. Get him and myself some tea. I'd bring him to the fairground and work there until midnight. My mum and stepdad worked there all day and night. I earned loads of cash and gave it all to my mum.

At fourteen, I went to live with my nanna because my mum left my stepdad, and moved in with another fella, who later became my second stepdad. I didn't know she'd moved in with him at the time, because no one ever told me. She dumped me and put my younger brother and sister into care. Our new stepdad didn't want us. By this time my sister had moved out of my nan's and was living on her own, she was pregnant. My older brother was in borstal. I never liked living with my nan. She was very strict. I just wanted my mum.

Again, I hated my new school. I started truanting. When I wasn't truanting it was holidays. I used to be picked up by the police all the time and dragged back to the school in a police car, with anyone else I used to bunk off with. We used to go and hide in the fields, in the bushes, at the end of the school pitches, even hide in the school itself.

I was watching the 'The Scarlet Pimpernel', and someone said, that happy-go-lucky, gay Pimpernel. I thought that gay meant happy. Then somebody said gay meant queer, bender, shirt-lifter and things like that. I'd heard of queer before – a poofter. I thought, that's what I am. Then I thought to myself, yes, I do find men attractive, but I am also sexually attracted to women.

Later on that year, still fourteen, I went back to live with my mum. She was pregnant. It was strange, my mum and my sister were pregnant at the same time. I bunked off regularly from my new school. One day, I was hiding in some flats. I knew a guy who lived there who was queer. I didn't know him. When he got home I asked him for a cup of tea because I was freezing. I didn't fancy him. I was curious. I said to him there was something different about him. He said his name was Martin and he was gay. I said, 'That's really good'. I still didn't know too much about what it meant. I went around there a lot after that.

When I was fifteen I had sex with a woman. She was about two years older than me. We were watching a big world concert with Bob Geldof. The next thing I knew I was grabbing her boobies. We were really into it. I was humping away. I thought I was up her, but I'd missed. I later found out her sister and my sister were watching us through the window while we were doing it. That was embarrassing.

The first guy I had sex with was one of Martin's friends. I was sixteen. I was round at Martin's place and he went out for a few minutes. A friend of his was round there and pounced on me and snogged me. He asked me out. I didn't know whether to. In the end I decided to. I went to the park to meet him and I thought that I didn't really want to do this. Then he took me back to his place, which was just round the corner from Debbie's. Then we had sex. I didn't know what you were supposed to do at first, then I loved it. We did it everywhere in his house.

It was this guy who told me to use condoms with other guys. Especially with Martin, as he had hepatitis and he said he was really dirty. He said that I didn't need to use them with him. I said, why not; he'd done things with Martin as well. All I knew about AIDS was the jokes.

Debbie must have found out and told my brother that I'd slept with this fella. My brother told my mum. I think she knew, and wished that I'd told her rather than my brother and the nasty way in which he told her. She reacted very badly and went on about 'poof', 'queer' – 'get out of my sight.' The worst thing was that she started shouting about it, and through those walls in those houses, everyone could hear. People got really nasty to me.

My second stepdad gave me a really hard time, saying that I must have AIDS because I was queer. That's when I decided to leave for London. I'd already left school because I hated it and didn't take my exams. I didn't like my YT [youth training] placement. There was a guy there giving me a really hard time, I'd punched him. I didn't get done because someone said he was antagonizing me.

I'd decided that I was much better than these people. By the time they were thirty they were on the dole, beating up their wives and drinking lager down the pub. I'd looked around at all the things that had happened around me in my life, and thought *I'm not going to end up like them.* I was going to improve myself and do something with my life.

My mum and stepdad didn't want me to leave because I was their unpaid babysitter. My brother was in London and sent me the money for my coach fare. I went to stay in his squat.

He was into drugs and had a record as long as your arm. Being very moral, I refused to take drugs when I was with him. I got various casual jobs and had enough money to live on. Then the police came to the door and he was done for burglary. I got done for helping him to escape, which wasn't true. Then some other people wrongly accused me of nicking money in the squat and so I moved out.

I moved into another squat in Peckham with Josh, who was a trans-vestite. I'd met him in a pub. Josh used to go out with men that paid him. I used to think that they were boyfriends giving him money to be kind. I had no idea about male prostitution. It never clicked until much later that he was a prostitute.

We used to go out and have some real fabby times. We used to get into Heaven free. That's where I did prostitution for the first time. I was seventeen, and didn't realize I was even doing it. I'd met this guy, about fifty, at the bar and he started buying me all these drinks. I was pissed. He asked me to come back to his place and he said he'd give me ninety quid. Josh said, 'Go on, do it, you might as well.'

I got back there and then he locked me in. I think he must have been ripped off before, and I must have looked the sort he didn't trust. We only had half an hour as he had to go and catch a plane. I was so pissed I kept falling off the bed and making him laugh. I had to give him a blow job and then I had to fuck him. I found the sex really interesting. I got a buzz. I'd never done anything like that before.

When he wasn't looking I nicked all his money and stuffed it down my knickers. Then as I was leaving, he accused me of nicking his money. He got really angry. Then I called a real bluff and said go on, search me then. He wouldn't prove it. I tried to kick in the front door. He let me out and I got a cab home. I got back and found I'd been burgled; all my clothes and belongings had gone.

Back home I used to wear things like white, tight trousers, jumpers and my hair was pretty long, like all the country boys. When I got to London, I dyed my hair black, wore black leather boots, black skin-tight trousers, black shirt, studded earrings with daggers on, necklaces and all the make-up went on. I used hair spray and spiked all my hair up.

Josh and I used to get really dressed up and go out to the Hippodrome. There we used to nick handbags, take the money and wallets, and put the rest back so they could be found. I didn't think it was fair to take passes, keys and things like that. I was too straight for my own good! After a while our faces started getting known and we decided we'd better not nick any more. Josh used to do business outside, he'd give them a blow job in the street and lift their wallets while he was doing it and we'd run off.

The next time I did prostitution was on my eighteenth birthday, in the girls' toilets at the Hippodrome. Josh told me to grab some geezer because he'd got loads of cash. I was really pissed and I could do and say things I wouldn't normally do. I'm normally really shy. He gave me £40. I was really disgusted with myself because I enjoyed it.

Just after my birthday, Josh and I fell out. I had already met these goths, punks and skins in Euston and went to stay in their squat.

I decided to take drugs just the once, for the sensation. We were at a party and someone said to me, here have some of this. It was speed. I loved the buzz so much I just kept on snorting it. Then we made 'bombs': we put some charlie [cocaine] into a liquorice [cigarette] paper, twisted it up and swallowed it. It explodes in your stomach and gives you a

152

buzz for twenty-four hours. Drugs just kept on appearing. I went on a complete head-fuck. Completely out of my brain. I went on doing that for six months. I must have got a week's sleep in that time.

I took acid, but had some really bad times. I wouldn't inject anything. It was suggested to me a million times. I can't stand anyone near me with a needle. I don't know where the money came from. I wasn't selling sex. I wouldn't sell drugs to anybody; I couldn't have lived with myself. I'm very moralistic like that. We partied all the time. Most of the time was spent in the dark, walking around by candle and lamp light. I lost loads and loads of weight. I hardly ever ate. All I drank was Pepsi and water. I became very rude and obnoxious.

When I was out, I used to get violent and caused loads of trouble. If anyone said anything to me, I'd kick their heads in. I used to think it was funny. I had loads of protection from the people in the squat. I used to hang around with people called Vomit, Slagger and psychopaths and nutters who'd come out of prison. I thought, yeah, I'm really into people.

After six months, I was in a mess. A friend who didn't touch drugs took me down to Brighton where she lived, to sort myself out. London had become too much of a rat-race. She watched me the whole time to make sure I didn't take anything. I got work down there in a bar. I came back a couple of months later.

I moved into a squat in Kentish Town. I worked for a short while as a dancer in Heaven. One night, while I was up on the pedestal and some guy was down on the floor, he put his hand up my ripped jeans. I told him to take his hand out. He decided to have himself a good feel and so I booted him in the face. He said he was going to get me. I thought no more about it. I left at three o'clock in the morning. I was knackered from dancing. I went down this alley towards Trafalgar Square, went up some steps and the next thing I knew three guys set on me. One of them was the guy who'd threatened me earlier.

They banged my head against the ground. They had a knife and gashed my neck open. They all raped me. They left me with my jeans completely ripped to shreds, my head and arse were gashed and bleeding. I was covered in bruises. I found my way to a friend's where I stayed for four months. I never left the apartment. It still has a traumatic effect on me. People say the way I was dressed, I asked for it.

I went back to the squat. I drifted back into drugs, on and off, for about a year. I spent most of my time sleeping, watching telly and going out at night.

There I met Dean, a guy who took me down to the Dilly and showed me prostitution on the street. I was nearly twenty by this time. I had to cut my hair and change my gothic appearance. I spent hours hanging around the Dilly at night gossiping with everyone – when I wasn't getting picked up.

I used to wear those clothes which would say *I'm a slut*. Ripped jeans where you could see almost the whole of my bum. Shirts that would say: look, my clothes can come off as simple as anything. I was provocative. I was an exhibitionist. I loved taking my clothes off in public. I only slept with people for money. I was very moral. I didn't sleep around with other people. As a rent boy, you can't have relationships. That, as far as I was concerned, was being unfaithful and was wrong.

I enjoyed the life, the adventure. You never knew what was going to happen. Going off with a stranger, closing your eyes and *jump*, see what happens. You risked your life every time you stepped out there. You didn't know where you were going to end up. You might get attacked, killed, arrested, anything could happen. I never used drugs when I was selling it, I had to be conscious. I always had to be drunk to do it, otherwise I was no good at it. I would be rude to the punters and tell them where to go. I was never scared, apart from the first couple of times.

When I first started, I worked out how much I needed for going out that night and maybe for the following night as well. I used to come up with a number of pounds I had to earn that night. As time went on, I'd just keep earning. I'd buy loads of drinks for everybody and chuck it around. I'd buy drugs.

When I was doing it, I'd always go back to somebody else's house. I'd find out who wasn't going to be in, and borrow their keys. I always made sure I was somewhere secure. I always liked to be indoors. I was never a toilet person, or 'pop around the corner and do it in the bushes' person.

I wasn't interested in most of my punters. I rarely got into social conversations with them. They don't want to talk to people who are intelligent or quick-witted. It frightens them if you have intelligent conversations. I had to pretend I was a dumb idiot. I just kept quiet and nodding to agree with them, and saying things like 'Really', 'You are so clever.' I used to think, 'God, how boring', 'Prat', 'That's bloody wrong'.

I had rules. I did basic stuff, both ways. I did hand jobs, blow jobs, humpty dump (penetrative sex). They were the three things that I would do with no problem. I had to be in complete control of my body, no matter what.

I did unsafe sex with certain people. I used to think I had an instinct about a person and that they wouldn't have HIV. I know it sounds stupid now. I've always thought that something out there was protecting me. I was really lucky how I got away without getting it. My HIV test three months ago was negative.

There's a lot of punters who are dirty bastards. They see a person under twenty and all they can think is that they want to shag them. They'd think that everybody wants to sleep with them. They are usually dirty, filthy and sweaty and don't bathe. I used to feel really dirty afterwards and would have to scrub myself inside out.

I found it easy to do, I'm bisexual anyway. It was a path in life I had to take. Maybe I'm psychologically unbalanced. I don't know. I was very rebellious. It was something that was totally taboo. I love doing things that are dangerous. I liked the money and the drinks.

Some were horrible. You just want to turn around and say, fuck off and die. You had all sorts of weird ones. I had one, he was about seventy, horrible-looking, but he seemed a nice person. But when I got back to his flat, he was vicious and nasty to me. He got me drunk, and started talking to me. He said his wife died a couple of years ago. Then he handed me a wig and a hat and this old lady's dress and asked me to put them on. He gave me this lipstick, and put it on me. Then he told me to follow him up the stairs. So far it was OK. Then he became a really strange person. He sat there staring and saying really strange things, strange head-fuck stuff. He'd talk to me as if I was his wife and call me by her name: he started talking about people he'd gone to bed with, then he'd say he was in charge because he was the master and had the money. It was weird.

The best one I did was a market trader. He was only about twenty-nine, from the East End. He came down to the Dilly, and said his wife had died, but he'd always been into fellows. I thought he was just a 'wham, bang, thank you ma'am' sort of person. So I got off with him in his car. He told me his son had to be put into care because he couldn't look after him. Then we got to this garage, I thought OK, here we go. He said, 'Can you put this on?'. It was a pageboy outfit. I'm six foot three, this guy is like five foot eight. I stood there with a little tutu, all-in-one frock thing on, with gloves, tights and a little hat. It was so funny. I couldn't laugh because this guy was really serious about it. That was camp. He kept saying things like, 'I've always wanted you.' I think his mind must have been really elsewhere. It was very weird. He wasn't rude or dirty or nasty. He was polite, friendly and stuff like that.

I was always well in touch with my mum. I phoned her every two or three days. If I had a lot on my mind, I'd ring her every day. She'd always ask me if I wanted her to come up to London. I'd always say no. I always wanted the security of my mum. She had protected me from everything. When I came to London she was still there. I used to go home from time to time. It was the only time I really ate. During the second year on the Dilly, I told her what I was doing. She said she knew. She was OK about it. I used to think she was psychic; she knew all sorts of things about us as kids.

I knew that, if anything went wrong, I could ask her to come and help me. I never did ask her. She was my security while I was on the streets. She knew for the last six years what I was really like. I often went back home to stay. Back to my own bedroom – my stuff was still there, that was security. When I came back to London, I was all refreshed. Even though there were always arguments, fights and silly things. That was what I'd known for my first sixteen years.

I didn't understand emotion. As a child I didn't have emotion. I cried, but that was because I'd fallen over. I couldn't handle emotion. That's why I don't have emotion. I was called the 'ice queen' because of it. When I was twenty, I met this girl, Sylvie, through a friend. I went out with her for about four months. I needed something. I gave her a lot of my feelings, but I wasn't emotional.

Then she told me she was pregnant. I really wanted to be a daddy. I wanted a baby. She moved in with me and my friend's squat. She used to go out with my friend hooking and going out to clubs, but I didn't mind as she was carrying my baby. I took her home to meet my mum, and we were going to get married.

Her and me used to have really aggressive sex. One night, after we'd had sex, she went running upstairs to my friend. He came rushing down and shouted to me, 'You've killed your baby, you've made her have a miscarriage, you bastard.' Then he took her to the hospital, and I was told that she'd refused to see me. Then both of them had nothing to do with me. I went off to stay with my friend in Brighton for a few days. I came back and another guy told me the truth about Sylvie. She carried his baby as well, and had lost it, just before I went out with her. He told me about how she'd used him.

I then found out she hadn't been pregnant at all, and had never gone to the hospital either. She had used me, taken me apart. She completely ruined my spirit. The person who I thought was my best friend had backed her against me. I couldn't get my head around it. I didn't laugh any more. I just lost it. I didn't know where the hell I was going or what I was doing. I ended up living in a dust hole underneath a block of flats. I'd sleep in the clothes I stood up in. Walking around the streets on my own, sitting in the park on my own, ignoring everyone.

After Sylvie, I knew I'd never sleep with another woman again. Not even to have my baby. I'd stick it in a bottle or something. I still fancy women sexually. I can find them really gorgeous.

Then I moved in to a drugs flat. A lot of things happened over a period of time. I can't be specific. I took smack and all sorts of drugs again. I also did a lot of thinking. I found out that some of the other guys I was close to were becoming HIV-positive. Some guys were getting killed, or ending up living with men as slaves. I was becoming frightened and thinking I ought to get out now, while I can. I didn't like the scene any more. There were a load of new boys on the Dilly causing trouble. I always knew that I had to come out of this at some time, and now was the time, I was twenty-one. I'd done what I wanted to do. I'd learnt what I needed to learn. It was time for me to start doing the things that I had to do next: getting somewhere to live and going to college.

I had a few regular punters, and started whittling them down until I ended up with one, Kevin, a thirty-year-old accountant. I stopped drugs. I cut down drinking to every two or three nights. I stopped chucking my money around. I could live on the money he gave me. I asked Kevin if I could live with him for six months, while I sorted myself out. He said yes. He gave me the security I needed: money and somewhere to live.

Shortly after I moved in, sex stopped because I'd met a boyfriend. I helped Kevin with his work. He gave me errand jobs to do, I answered the phone and did some typing. Our relationship was distant. We had separate bedrooms and we didn't really communicate, which suited me.

I got the help I needed to find out about courses and colleges from Streetwise. I did the rest myself, it was very difficult. Out there in the other world, off the rent, I thought I was dumb. I assumed that I was not speaking correctly, or thinking correctly. I thought I was in the wrong situation at the time, for all sorts of things. I needed someone to put things in the right order, and say, OK, we'll deal with this and then this, and we'll put it all together and package it up.

I was going to college and I wanted my mum to be proud of me. I wanted her to see all the good things about me and make her really proud. The day I had my interview and was told that I'd been accepted on to the course, she died. I was going down to see her in hospital that evening, and I'd planned to surprise her, if my interview was successful. But she'd died that morning of cancer, two hours before I went to the interview. I had to go to my interview knowing she'd just died. I felt really guilty because she'd been saying for ages she wanted to come and visit me. I didn't know how ill she was. No one in the family told me anything.

There were many times when I nearly resigned on my two-year child care course. I thought the work was hard and knackering. I used to be up until 3.00 or 4.00 am. Then into college for 8.30 am to 4.30 pm. Then I'd sit in the library until 8.30 pm. No matter what, I had to get through.

I'd just found out about my dyslexia. I had to re-read everything constantly. Many times I thought I couldn't do it. I couldn't work out one word from another. I couldn't figure out sentences, anything. I was crying a lot of the time. I'd never dealt with any of my grief. But I got through, and got a job out of London straight away. Kevin was no help at all throughout this time, he had no idea about encouraging me.

Not long after I'd started my course, I was very drunk in a nightclub. I went and sat down because I was knackered and I thought I'd have another drink. This guy Nick came up and just started chatting to me. I said, do you want to marry me then, and stupid things like that. He said the thing that he found most interesting about me was that I didn't say, 'Let's go back to your house and have a good shag.' I'd said, 'No, I'll meet you tomorrow' and gave him my phone number.

Nick gave me security. He had the patience I'd never seen in anybody before. I never thought I'd find the patience that he had. The crap that I came out with and he stood it. I'd go into really stroppy moods all the time. I'd be abusive. I'd be angry with him. I'd want to go out clubbing all the time, say to him, fuck off you are not coming out. I'd ring him up at two in the morning, pissed as a fart, going blah, blah, blah.

Now three years on, I'm living with him, away from London, feeling very secure with him. He was my security during my course, and still is. I got a job in child care straight after I passed my exams and have been working for eighteen months.

I was always sexually frigid. That's why I got drunk. When I was drunk, I had no inhibitions. It was the only way I could have sex. I never actually got to explore my sexuality. It wasn't there in my mind. I'm now starting to get to the point where I'm starting to feel safe with sex. I'm secure and more confident in myself.

I don't know what my sexuality is. I still have things towards women, very particular women. They have to be tall and very intelligent. Strong powerful women were my role models: Marlene Dietrich, Diana Rigg and my mum. Women are astute. Men are like their fathers or how society has made them.

I had no male role models. I knew who I *didn't* want to be like: my dad, both my stepdads, my older brother, any of the men I ever knew.

I'm not ashamed of what I was. If I hadn't done what I've done, I wouldn't be as happy as I am now. I think otherwise I would have always been innocent. I had to go through all that. I wouldn't know as much about people as I do. I know more than most people. I can read between the lines, where a lot of people can't. I understand when someone is lying. I pick up vibes off people, like being nervous, all sorts of things.

A lot of people have gone through life: they go to college, or leave home, go to work, blah, blah, blah and that's it. But I've had the widening experience. I've done the drugs, the alcohol, sex with women, sex with men, the streets, violence. I have a very old head on young shoulders from what I know. My path in my life gave me that.

I am very close to my younger half-sister. I want to make sure she gets better than me. It has just come out that my second stepdad has been sexually abusing her for years. It's sick and causing me a lot of worry.

One day, I think the effects of my past are going to come out. I'm going to have a breakdown. I want to postpone it until I'm more secure and better able to deal with it. I know I haven't dealt with the problems in my head. They keep piling up. I have a lot of pressure inside of me.

I can't believe what I used to do. I couldn't do it now. I remember everything, and think, is that really my past? I think I must have protective spirits, to have got through what I have.

In Conclusion

The life stories in this book are told using the interviewees' own words and were recorded in 1993 and 1994.

From 1988 to 1993, I worked at the original Streetwise Youth, the first UK charity dedicated to supporting male and trans youth who sold sex on the streets. As the specialist HIV and AIDS worker, I had developed a relationship of trust with these young adults that later enabled me to capture these rare, frank interviews. Because they had unlimited time to tell their stories, the individuals I spoke with gave me deeper insights into their lives than they had previously disclosed at Streetwise.

Like all children and young people, they needed love, trust, respect, physical and emotional care, appropriate attention and guidance, praise and security. Sadly, most of the youths I worked with had, as children, been neglected and/or abused by their primary caregivers. Most had unhappy childhoods. They felt deprived and rejected. As a result, they lacked confidence and self-worth. If they knew their parents, they had poor and unhappy relationships with them. It seemed to make little difference whether or not they came from single-parent or two-parent families, or whether they had financially stable backgrounds.

Zoe's (formerly Jason) childhood story contrasts with the others. She told me that she had received the care and nurture she'd needed from her mother and sisters. As a result, she appeared to be the most stable and emotionally secure of all of the interviewees. The security she found from her loving and trusted relationship with a parent was

161

unusual, when compared to the family circumstances of most of the individuals I have worked with.

This conclusion was agreed with the interviewees who were still alive at the time of writing in 1994. There were common factors which led to their marginalized, maligned and criminalized lifestyles – caused through little fault of their own. Nevertheless, many of them often ended up shouldering the guilt. I refer, of course, only to those subjects for whom selling sex was not something they wanted to engage in but nevertheless ended up doing so for various reasons.

Childhood experiences

Role models

The interviewees' experiences and associations with differing male and female role models left them with profound confusion in their relationships to adults, especially adult men. In all of the individuals' stories, there was no example of a father, surrogate father or significant male who had been a 'good' role model, offering love, guidance, time and emotional security. From their perspectives, men were seen as only good for providing money and creature comforts in exchange for sex. In other words, men could not be trusted.

Their early and ongoing experiences with men left them feeling disempowered, unless 'rewards' were involved. In addition, punters came from all walks of life. These young adults' perceptions of men were also likely to be extended to *all* men, including those trying to help them such as those in caring roles, potential partners and friends. Since their trust was betrayed early on in their lives, the development of genuine trust with men later on became difficult to achieve.

This fact was reinforced by all their accounts, in various ways. Ryan and Paul wished that they had fathers; they thought this would have solved their emotional difficulties. Both suffered rejection and further disempowerment when their respective stepfathers arrived on the scene.

Madser, Adam and Zoe's (step)fathers were both emotionally and physically absent from their lives. In the brief time that Simone knew her father, he rejected her way of being. In addition, her only confidante turned out to be her abuser. It is hardly surprising she had an ambivalent attitude towards men. She sought out their company, but when she got close to them, they let her down. However, through selling sex, she appeared to take away their power and gain it for herself. She had little respect for men. Even caregivers disempowered her. She was typical of these young people in general, in that her view of men was largely negative.

I was very much aware of my own gender whilst working with these clients. They seemed to seek out a 'mothering' role from me. Indeed, mothers appear to have been very much 'present' in their lives, in contrast to the absent fathers. They tended to have had emotionally intense, albeit seemingly neglectful, relationships with their mothers. In many cases they tried to gain their approval at all costs. Mothers were put on a pedestal and idolized.

As adults, they were forgiving of how their mothers had behaved towards them as children, and understanding of their mothers' situations at the time. On reflection, they understood that their mothers were having their own difficulties in coping with life. However, they blamed themselves for these difficulties. For some, their relationship with their mothers appeared to have reinforced negative perceptions of their own masculinity. For example, Paul's mother used to tell him that men were good only for money and sex.

The arrival of stepfathers on the scene seemed to have enhanced this belief. As boys, they felt further alienation from their mothers. They viewed the new man as a rival for their mothers' attentions and felt powerless because their individual roles as 'the man about the house' had been usurped.

Both Madser and Ryan were subjected to considerable emotional and physical abuse from their mothers, resulting in the development of 'eager to please' mechanisms to try to stop the beatings. Madser's story illustrates this: 'At the age of seven … I was learning to try to please me ma, because there was less chance of getting a slap. Me ma wasn't a very good cook and I started cooking for the family. I used to cook childish things … I learned to check the roast in the oven. I was never thanked for doing it, I think it was appreciated but I still got beaten.'

Madser's comfort came from his brothers and sister. They were protective of him. It may be that because he was able to form positive relationships with his siblings, he was able to make friendships with others. Yet his life's trajectory seemed almost doomed from the start, because of his perceived sense of rejection by his mother. Gambling, drugs, alcohol, sex, violence and his enormous willpower aided him in 'blanking things out', so he could deal with almost anything that life presented to him. He lived for the moment, always in the present. He was a fighter to the end, always trying to defy his mother's message to him, 'I'll make you regret the day you were born, you evil bastard.'

From Ryan's account, he seemed only to see gloom in life. His mother's violent and rejecting treatment of him was reinforced by her disciplinarian religion. In consequence, he feared all black women. Ryan found little comfort from anyone, not even his relatives. As a child and as an adult, he felt as though he was completely on his own. In addition, he received no support for the considerable racial discrimination he experienced, or for his physical disability. He was totally isolated and felt utterly worthless. As an adult his needs were simply 'to belong' and to be accepted as himself.

Paul, on the contrary, had all the love he needed from his nan. But when he was young and inexplicably separated from her, it left him perplexed, wandering and searching for love. He was neglected. His mother was either out at work or with the stepfather, rather than Paul. He thought sex meant that someone loved you. Thus, he used sex to get love and he came to conflate the two. When referring to his drug use, he said, 'I was like a kid with sweets,' and these were clearly his 'rewards' and played a part in escaping from his pain. When he finally left home, he was able to go back and establish good relationships with his mother and his nan. After a subsequent return home following his diagnosis of HIV, he was able to show his anger at his mother's earlier neglect of him. Her acceptance of their real past seems to have played a large part in the beginning of a close relationship.

Adam's mother also let him down when, from the age of seven, he was presented with various stepfathers. He felt rejection at his particular time of need, when he was subjected to sexual and physical abuse by his uncle. He could not count on his mother's support when he saw that her alliances, as always, were clearly with the abuser and with his stepfather's family. He turned his back on everything, determined to better himself and be nothing like those he'd left behind. Again, like Paul, only by his leaving home could his mother become more accessible to him. Via phone calls, Adam was at last able to get her undivided attention, prior to her premature death.

Of all of the interviewees, only Zoe (formerly Jason) had a positive nurturing relationship with her mother. This was further reinforced by positive relationships with her sisters, all of whom she idolized. They affirmed her trans identity, allowing her to view it with clarity and strength. Her later choice in turning to sex work was her way of acquiring further strength, power, and money to help her achieve the various goals in her life.

Simone's (as Simon) main contact with females was through her foster mother and care workers. She said she enjoyed the emotional closeness she was able to get from female care workers. Yet she did not seek out other female company. She had very little contact with women, knew little about them.

Simone's experiences with all adults – foster carers, social workers, residential care home workers – played a transitory part in her life. She never felt like she had a sense of permanence with anyone, or had been able to find security anywhere. Everything she liked had failed. Not surprisingly she found solace in the 'love drug' (ecstasy), which acted like a cushion, until that started to let her down too, as it ceased to provide her with the escape she needed. Her true feelings came through, resulting in many attempts to take her own life – her cry for help.

Reflecting on my experiences with these young people, each one of them had very different beliefs about women versus men. They often expected women to be nurturing, whereas their relationships with men were more obstructive or challenging.

Disruptive childhood behaviour

In their stories, the interviewees described their childhood distress as having been regularly expressed through disruptive behaviour, both in and out of school. They often did this to seek attention, to express their frustrations and anger at home. Their disruptive behavioural patterns isolated them not only from their teachers, but also from their peers. They were vulnerable to bullying from their families, peers and teachers. They frequently lacked the ability to concentrate in school and their learning suffered as a result. Frustration followed – and ultimately, truancy. Most of the people I worked with had poor literacy and numeracy skills, which resulted in poor employment prospects.

Childhood sexual experiences

These individuals had largely learned about sex from paedophiles at a very young age. They described these experiences as 'normal'. Their perceptions, together with their feelings of whether or not the experiences were pleasurable, does not necessarily coincide with an observer's perceptions of what is morally right.

Truanting frequently afforded the opportunity for the youths to engage in petty crime and also made them vulnerable to sexual abuse. They all responded differently to the abuse. Zoe (as Jason) and Paul did not see it as abuse at all. They saw it as the welcome attention of a stranger offering friendship, companionship, a sexual adventure and the reward of money. Although they felt guilty after engaging in sexual activity for the first time, they went on to seek out further sexual adventures, enjoying the financial and – in Paul's case – also the emotional rewards it brought; an unwitting entry into prostitution.

In both cases, the family found out and called in the police. Both Zoe and Paul said they resented this action, both wanting to protect their abusers and continue with their new-found adventures and the rewards which gave them previously unknown feelings of self-worth and power. Later in life, neither believed that these incidents had any sort of harmful effects on them. To them, it was not sexual abuse. Would their early, happy sexual experiences have been perceived as so pleasant, if the rewards had not been forthcoming? Or, were they youngsters exploring their sexuality, regardless of their rewards?

However for others, such as Madser and Adam, their first sexual experiences, at the age of ten, were very unpleasant. There was no question of any consent. They did not receive any emotional or financial rewards. Both knew their abusers prior to the time of the abuse and both were left with feelings of contempt and hate towards them, feeling powerless to do anything about it.

Madser was truanting at the time of his first sexual abuse. He had no one to talk to, because he was afraid of getting into trouble if he divulged what had happened. He also said that he had so much else going on in his life, that compared with the beatings he was receiving, it paled into insignificance. By contrast, Adam was off school sick. Like most children, he felt safe in his own home. When his uncle broke in and violently abused him, Adam believed that his mother would take the side of the abuser, as she had when another child had reported sexual abuse from the same man. Both Madser and Adam had needed someone to confide in, but knew no one.

Apart from their partners, I was the first person Madser and Adam had spoken to in depth about their abuse. Neither of them regarded these abusive incidents as 'sexual' experiences, they were viewed as 'something else'. They did not have the vocabulary to describe these ordeals.

Simone said her experience was very different. For Simon, as he was then, between the ages of five and fourteen, the man who was his only trusted friend and comforter was also a sexual partner. To Simon it was a 'normal', gentle, caring experience. There was no concept that this sexual component of the relationship may have been harmful. The trauma came later when they were separated, and the abuser was imprisoned. No one had considered Simon's perception of the situation or the grief he was going through. Only later in counselling, as Simone the adult, had she realised her only trusting relationship had been a total sham. Yet this was not how it seemed at the time. She experienced huge inner turmoil and no longer understood who she could trust, or who to turn to. She also believed that her trans identity was linked to her earlier sexual experiences and as a result was 'imposed on her' – unlike Zoe. Zoe and her mother were conscious of her differences when Zoe was still young and this seems to affirm her emergence as a trans woman.

Money

To all the contributors, in this book, with the exception of Ryan, money represented power. You could have fun. You could go out. You could spend it on drugs. You could spend it on hormones and surgery. You give this service to your punter and you get money. It seemed straightforward – unlike their experiences of relationships with people.

The 'dance' in getting the money was often a devious and dangerous game. The highs and lows were addictive. It was a gamble and an adventure, in which the stakes were their bodies and their minds. For many of them, the cash obtained in this way was not spent on practical needs such as getting accommodation and saving up for the future. They told me that, as soon as they got hold of the money, they quickly got rid of it, because it was seen as 'dirty'. Large sums could be spent on drugs, alcohol and gambling to block out the pain of their past and current circumstances. Many said they needed drugs and alcohol to be able to sell sex. But then they needed to sell sex to buy the drugs and alcohol. Another quick way to dispose of their money was to buy lots of drinks for people in clubs, in a bid to show how successful they had been. This used to annoy Ryan, as he made very little money at all.

Staying in a club all night meant that there was no need to find a punter, sleep in the street or beg for a floor to kip on. In such situations, individuals questioned the point in keeping hold of their money when they might be dead tomorrow. In general, it seemed difficult for some of them to think beyond the present day.

Punters

Punters came from every profession, every sector of society and sought out a wide variety of experiences. Some actively looked for sex with young-looking boys. One could not tell who a punter was just by looking at them. Public perceptions reinforced the stereotype that they were all gay men; this was clearly not the case. They told the young men, for example, that they were heterosexual and married; having 'a bit' before going home from work. They clearly didn't acknowledge being homosexual in any way.

There was a lot of pressure for the youths to look as young as possible. The younger they were, the more physically and emotionally under-developed they appeared, the more they were in demand. They had a 'sell-by date'. After that, new younger youths arrived on the scene, and there was little demand for the older-looking ones.

Some of these punters held positions of power and influence in society. I recall a youth telling me about his experience of having been charged with importuning (soliciting) and being sentenced in court by the judge – who had recently paid for sex with him. It is ironic how society criminalizes these young adults in an effort to make itself look responsible for 'cleaning up crime'. Every young person I met wanted to sort out their problems and be in a position where they could actively choose whether to sell sex or not.

'I got beaten up a lot of times. I was forced to have sex and I was ripped off. People had sex with me while I was asleep, I was abused loads of times.' This was Paul's story, but it could be that of many young men selling sex, for whom abuse was commonplace in both their professional and private lives. For many of them, violence had been a common theme. They may not even have viewed their assault as abuse or rape. They blamed themselves for their lifestyles and viewed such occurrences as yet another consequence they must endure. They experienced deep trauma, humiliation, anger and distress, resulting in long-term problems. They did not expect any support or protection. They were unable to go to the police because their lifestyles were criminalized. They believed they would not be treated sympathetically.

It was important that after violence and rape, that they should have had support and a medical examination to check and treat any external and internal injury. They were also at risk of sexually transmitted diseases and HIV, although few of them seem to have realized this. They endured considerable physical and emotional pain. When self-worth was so low, drugs and alcohol were used as a coping mechanism. When things got too much, some of the individuals attempted suicide – and tragically, some of these attempts were successful.

Racism

Some of these young people experienced racism on the grounds of their skin colour, exacerbating their problems over and above those already stated here. They were more visible on the streets and in the bars that were predominantly frequented by white people. They encountered racism from their peers, punters, police and the public.

For many, to be male meant the expectation to be 'macho', masculine and 'very heterosexual'. If they were unable to behave according to the (heterosexual) norms of their community they may encounter fierce prejudice from within it, particularly with response to sexual preference and behaviour. .

In addition to the everyday racism they faced, punters sought out these youngsters to act out various humiliating scenarios. The men who frequented the central London pick-up venues were nearly all white. Ryan, an African-Caribbean young man, was sought out to engage in power games relating to black slavery, humiliation and being the macho black 'stud'. South-East Asian youths could be expected to act out submission, femininity and passivity. Some also endured these expectations from partners in their private lives. It is not surprising that these young people often felt more isolated than their white peers and suffered extreme feelings of low self-esteem.

Trans women

Trans women faced transphobia, homophobia and sexism both on and off the streets, wherever they went. Some, like Simone who was black, also experienced racism. They were ridiculed, ostracized and misunderstood merely for being who they were. Most employers held such prejudices too – on the whole, trans people had few job prospects.

They were under pressure to look and behave in a 'convincing' way. There were few places where they could be safe and feel safe. Some young trans women were introduced to Streetwise by the young men already attending and they welcomed the drop-in environment. Here they were accepted and found the support for, and validation of, who they were and how they wanted to be.

Simone and Zoe vividly described some of the predicaments they faced, both in their private lives and in selling sex. I highlight here some general areas that affected trans women at the time.

Access to NHS healthcare was problematic. Many trans women were unable to access GP and other services, their concerns were not understood by them. However, some trans people could find general healthcare services that accommodated for, and understood their needs, from projects such as Streetwise Youth and other organizations working with sex workers, homeless people and drug users. Here, they also could receive appropriate advice about safe sex and how to reduce their risks to violence in male, trans or female sex work. What was lacking in these organizations, however, were peer and mentor support and networks.

Many of the trans women either had to work as 'boys' in male pick-up environments or as women in female ones. Working as a male meant having to perform abhorrent sexual activities alien to their female nature, hiding their breasts and other female characteristics. Working as a female meant some had to hide their penises and anything that could be construed as male. They had to become mistresses of deception and hope they would not be 'sussed'. Being exposed could mean being thrown out of a car in the middle of nowhere, or worse – exposed to rape and other forms of physical violence.

Over time, Simone and Zoe moved away from selling sex on the streets to living and working alone in a safer environment: for Simone, her boyfriend lived in her flat and was out all day; for Zoe, her own apartment. They advertised their services in newspapers, windows and through trans agencies. They made their own appointments using a land-line. There was no internet or any smartphones at that time and so they could not conduct work through apps like today. Simone was popular and had many customers advertising herself, in her words, as a 'chick with a dick'. She saved for breast enhancement and regular hormone treatment. At that time, she was labelled with the now outmoded term 'pre-op' – the expectations were that for a trans woman to be complete, she must have the lower surgery and become 'post-op' – also now an outmoded term and expectation. Today, individuals can be freer to express, or not express, their gender and identity as they wish; for example, as a trans woman or as non-binary. Simone was as content with her body as she was with her trans identity, referring to herself as 'transsexual' – the word of that time.

One considerable stress, for both Simone and Zoe, was accessing medical services for hormone treatment and gender enhancing surgery. Pursuing these options would have meant waiting at least five to seven years for an assessment with the NHS gender identity clinic, a process that reinforced sexist stereotypes of 'how to be a woman,' such as wearing pencil skirts, heels and lots of make-up. Such delays led to young trans women developing adult male characteristics, causing long-term psychological harm and making treatments less effective. The only way a trans woman could feel aligned with her body and speed the process up was to seek an alternative route. Word of mouth led Zoe and Simone to a private consultant psychiatrist with an excellent reputation for assessment, who had respect for their chosen gender – something almost unique within the medical profession at that time. However, with this kind of expertise came a hefty price. They had to pay for regular hormone prescriptions, as well as for the surgery costs – in the thousands – placing an extra burden on their financial lives and additional pressures on their sex work.

Zoe advertised herself as female and had plenty of business. She saved £3000 for upper surgery and £7000 for lower surgery, and she was 'over the moon'. But she worked in isolation, at risk of violence. There were no apps like the ones that exist today, which have safety mechanisms to reduce the risk of violence. National Ugly Mugs, for example, is a UK-wide charity that works with sex workers to create, share and deliver resources that help to keep them safe. I was later to learn that the event every sex worker feared the most had happened to Zoe. Tragically, she was found dead in her bed after being with an 'ugly mug' punter.

Legal issues

There were many contradictions in the law. In 1993 and 1994 when these recordings were made, some laws served to criminalize these young adults, others to protect them. However, in practice, the laws that were supposed to protect them often didn't.

The Children Act 1989 s.17(1) placed important duties on local authorities to provide a range of services for 'children' under eighteen who were 'in need' and whose welfare was likely to be seriously affected without these services. The theme that ran through the Act was that the needs of the child are paramount.

If a young person under eighteen came to the attention of the social services, the Children Act gave powers for investigations to be made with a view to promoting the welfare of the child. Good practice meant that social services could provide the child and family with a range of appropriate services, such as family counselling. In practice, however, the parent was first notified of the young person's whereabouts and normally agreed to have him or her returned home. The young person was returned to the very same situation he or she had found intolerable in the first place. The parents and youngsters referred were unlikely to welcome an investigation into family matters.

Some local authorities would only investigate if a young person reported that they were suffering significant harm. It was most unlikely that they would make such a complaint, given that they risked ending up in care. Some ran away from home and, when they were found, the local authority, via the courts, made the decision as to whether the youngster should be taken into care or sent home.

If the individual had been returned home, they had learned the system. The next time they ran away, they tried to beat it. All of these young people, regardless of age, would have been driven underground to avoid police and social services intervention. In this situation, they were extremely vulnerable and believed the only way to survive was through crime and selling sex. Some drifted into whosoever's bed or floor they could secure. They were often exploited.

However, local authorities did have the powers to accommodate young homeless people aged sixteen and seventeen, if this would have safeguarded their welfare. But the interpretation of 'in need' was entirely at the discretion of the local authority, and was usually the decision of an individual social worker. A Centrepoint survey of London's social services found that three-quarters of departments claimed not to have enough accommodation to meet young homeless people's needs: 37 per cent of the departments did not even have the housing provision needed for young people already in their care.

Rather than the police arresting these youngsters, the Children Act 1989 s.46(1) gave the police powers to intervene if any child or young person under the age of eighteen came to their attention and was seen to be 'at risk'. They could have taken them into their protection for seventy-two hours, ascertained the young person's wishes and referred them on to a refuge or alternative local authority accommodation. Then they could have investigated with a view to safeguarding the young person's welfare. In practice, however, sixteen- and seventeen-year-olds were often not interpreted as being 'at risk'. This was because they were legally free to leave home and were no longer required to be in full-time education. Leaving home was seen to be the young person's choice.

Yet, selling sex in this way was one of the riskiest occupations there was. The individual was at risk of physical and sexual assault, exploitation and serious ill health. Many of these exploited young people were not regarded as needing protection. They were seen as 'encouraging men for immoral purposes' and viewed as abusers of the law and thus criminalized.

Under three different statutes, the law stated that a person seen to be compelling, inciting and assisting a child under the age of eighteen to stay away from a 'responsible person' was committing a custodial offence. This was to protect the young person from exploitation. It affected the way in which organizations were able to work with young people, as they could be seen as keeping the young person away from the 'responsible person'. This made it tricky for them to both protect and work legally with these under-eighteen-year-olds in England and Wales, and under-sixteen-year-olds in Scotland.

A handful of voluntary organizations, such as Centrepoint and The Children's Society, *did* work with these youngsters. Such organizations had to be registered with the Department of Health in order to provide a refuge or other accommodation to under-eighteen-year-olds who appeared to be at risk of harm. In practice, a ten-year-old child could be referred there. Few runaways knew about them or understood how to access these facilities unless they found an advocate to help them. In practice, there were few available places in these refuges when compared with the number of young people who sought help.

The Children Act gave the power to local authorities to act positively with under-eighteen-year-olds in terms of provision of housing, care and support. Streetwise saw many who should have been, but were not, provided for under this legislation.

Alternative legal income

There was no legal source of income available to sixteen and seventeen-year-olds. In September 1988, entitlement to benefits was withdrawn unless the individual was on a youth training scheme. Such places were not guaranteed and could be virtually impossible to secure. Therefore, without the prerequisite accommodation, these people were denied access to benefits. Without accommodation they were unable to obtain legal employment, so in order to survive many resorted to criminal means.

The age of criminal responsibility

The Children and Young Persons Act 1933 s.50 (as amended by the Children and Young Persons Act 1963 s.16(1)) stated that no child under the age of ten could be found guilty of an offence. Much debate occurred on whether children between ten and fourteen could be criminally responsible. On 17 March 1995, the House of Lords allowed an appeal stating that they were incapable of committing an offence unless there was proof that the child knew that what they were doing was seriously wrong, as opposed to being merely naughty or mischievous. A young person of fifteen and over was subjected to the same rules as an adult. Those under eighteen were treated as children if they needed protection, but if they were not given proper protection then these same children – the fifteen to seventeen-year-olds – could be criminalized as adults.

Rape

Surprisingly, male rape was only recognized by law in 1994. Before that time, rape was defined as non-consensual vaginal intercourse that took place with a woman by a man. Equal status has now been given to heterosexual and homosexual sexual assault and the definition broadened.

During the time when these youths were selling sex, where rape was concerned, both male and female trans sex workers had no protection from the law. If they found Streetwise, they were offered crisis counselling and ongoing support, as well as access to medical help for any physical injuries. However, many had nowhere to go. These sex workers were considered by many to be 'fair game' for non-consensual activities. The reality was that, even after 1994, if the sexual histories of the sex workers had been brought out in a courtroom, there likely would have been great difficulty in convicting a rapist, given the prejudice that existed.

Consent

During my time at Streetwise Youth, the age of male homosexual sexual consent was twenty-one. Most of the people I worked with were under the age of consent. In the eyes of the law, if either party was under the age of consent, both were liable to prosecution. In 1994, consent was changed to eighteen and it wasn't until 2001 that it was further reduced to sixteen, in line with opposite-sex couples. This posed considerable

176

difficulties for agencies in providing meaningful education and support to those under the age of consent.

Soliciting and importuning

It was not illegal to be a male prostitute. Nor is it now. But it was, and still is, illegal to ply your business. The legislation referred to in the accounts of Paul, Simone and Zoe, and which was commonly applied to other young adults I worked with, was the Sexual Offences Act 1956, s.32 which states, 'It is an offence for a man persistently to solicit or importune in a public place for immoral purposes.' The term 'man' also applied to a boy subject to the criminal age of responsibility. The word importune is no longer used. A trans person was charged according to the sex on their birth certificate. Here 'immoral purposes' referred to some kind of sexual activity and was applied to a man soliciting either a man or a woman. 'Persistently' meant two separate acts of importuning and interpreted as two invitations to the same person. The penalty was either a fine or a custodial sentence, the latter of which would have implications for future employment opportunities for the youths.

Some injustices were reported: Paul recounted that he was arrested while his punter was dismissed, Simone said that she wasn't picking up a man and yet she was still charged. Zoe and Simone both recalled that if the police couldn't charge them with importuning they were arrested for highway obstruction.

Highway Obstruction

The Highways Act 1980, s.137 states, 'If a person, without lawful authority or excuse, in any way wilfully obstructs the free passage along a highway, he is guilty of an offence liable to a fine.' It was common for these youths to be charged with – and fined for this offence.

Fines

These young adults had no legal income. Yet the criminal justice system imposed fines even where it was quite apparent that they could not be paid for only by selling sex, or not paid at all. The result was a warrant for non-payment of fines, which could result in a period in custody. While Simone was under social services' care, she ended up in a youth detention centre four times for non-payment of fines.

Surviving against the odds during the HIV epidemic

During my years at the project, there was virtually no support in the United Kingdom for young men and trans women selling sex on the streets. It was ironic that those who were most at risk of harm were the least resourced. Mainstream health and social service providers recognized the need for HIV services for marginalized groups, but deemed the subject matter 'too hot to handle' owing to the taboo nature of our clients having sex with men, or being trans, and selling sex. They also did not wish to be seen to condone illegal, underage sex between men under the age of 21. The age of consent for sex between men posed problems for mainstream institutions for the delivery of meaningful, explicit HIV health promotion at that time, using culturally appropriate language and graphics.

The limited HIV funding at this time allowed for more alternative organizations, such as charities, to apply for funding that would extend to 'hard to reach groups', such as to sex workers, to homeless people, and drug users, so that the organization could provide the most appropriate HIV health promotion and support. The aim was to reduce the risk of transmitting HIV and other sexually transmitted infections for individuals in groups that were seen to be at higher risk of infection.

Unlike now, there were no targeted health resources available to trans people at that time. We worked closely with a trans woman volunteer (Michelle Ross) from the Terrence Higgins Trust in London, who was a great role model and supported our work with the young trans women.

Even with this funding, it was for HIV services only. Fortunately, we had a very good reputation with our statutory funders, who recognised our crucial work. Finding additional funding was difficult, but we were lucky in that our founder, Father Bill Kirkpatrick, had good connections.

These young people knew how to look after themselves in terms of reducing their risks of HIV infection. They took the condoms and lubricants that were freely available in the day centre and from the outreach workers on the streets. The project continuously facilitated spontaneous group and one-to-one sessions for everyone in both settings. In the latter days, a pioneering peer education programme was running, too. Nevertheless, for many, contracting HIV and its longer term consequences paled into insignificance when weighed against their more immediate survival concerns. Rape and violence were common. There were pressures from both paying and non-paying partners to engage in unsafe sexual practices. When combined with the natural reaction of losing one's sensibilities 'in the heat of the moment', putting safer sex into practice was tricky. Sadly some, like Madser and Paul, contracted HIV and later died as a result.

At this time, contracting HIV was considered a death sentence. HIV and AIDS medication was in its infancy and had considerable, unpleasant, side effects. Some at that time chose not to take it at all. The advent of PrEP was still thirty years away. Unlike today, medications were only prescribed after the person had developed AIDS and with this, many people did not survive.

I have to admire the remarkable qualities of the six people I interviewed and many others who worked the streets amidst an HIV and AIDS epidemic. They were not given the opportunities in life that most people had. Their circumstances were such that they had to leave home at a very young age. Some, like Paul, Adam and Madser, showed enormous strength and courage in leaving behind everything they knew, and moving to London when they recognized that they had no hope at home.

Few of them had supportive friends or relatives. They were quite alone. They 'coped' with feeling scared, lonely, depressed and suicidal by themselves. They developed great initiative in finding places to sleep, and they learned to deal with exploitative people. They had no legal entitlements to money, yet somehow they found money to live. They handled living with violence and sexual assault. They experienced complex sexual identity problems arising from the mixture of sexual abuse, selling their bodies, as well as their own emerging sexual identities, and for Zoe and Simone, their emerging trans identities too. They lived in an environment where even the law offered little protection; there was only hostility and condemnation of their presence. In spite of this they needed to survive, to carry on and make lives for themselves, whilst dealing with their inner demons. Sometimes their ways of dealing with life's problems worked for them, sometimes they did not. They learned to grow up with no one to guide them and against the odds.